The
Cuckoo Line

Kevin Robertson

www.crecy.co.uk

ISBN 9781909328570

First published in 2016 by Crécy Publishing Ltd

Publisher's note: Every effort has been made to identify and correctly attribute photographic credits. Any error that may have occurred is entirely unintentional.
In line with the new design the front cover image has changed from that originally advertised. All other information is unaffected.

Printed in Slovenia by GPS Group

Crécy Publishing Limited
1a Ringway Trading Estate
Shadowmoss Road
Manchester M22 5LH

www.crecy.co.uk

Front Cover top:
Reported as the 9.05am 'Special Freight' north from Polegate, the train is seen here near Horam behind Brighton-based unrebuilt 'Battle of Britain' No 34055 Fighter Pilot on 2 July 1960.
J. J. Smith, courtesy Bluebell Railway Museum

Front Cover bottom:
'E5' 0-6-2T No 32588 with three potential revenue-earning wagons in tow. The small goods yard behind is dominated by coal traffic, the receiving merchants being required to empty the wagons within a specified length of time or pay a 'demurrage' (storage) charge.
J. J. Smith, courtesy Bluebell Railway Museum

Rear Cover:
The LCGB 'Wealdsman' railtour of 13 June 1965. Seen at the Heathfield photographic stop, this part of the tour was in charge of 'Moguls' Nos 31803 and 31411. Officially the line had closed the previous day although freight would continue to Heathfield until 1968.
Roger Thornton

Title page:
On a wet 1 September 1951, the Hospital electric locomotive crosses a minor road near to Hellingley station with what is probably an empty coal wagon.
J J Smith, Bluebell Railway Museum

Contents

Acknowledgements and Bibliography

A number of references have been sourced in the compilation of this book, both published and archived. In addition, a great number of individuals have been kind enough to offer support, without which little would have been possible.

To start with, mention must be made of Nikki Favell, manager of the bookshop at Sheffield Park on the Bluebell Railway. It was she who suggested the idea for this book in the first place – so who am I to disagree with a lady? Then there is Tony Hillman from the Bluebell Museum, who kindly made accessible the vast number of images taken by the late J. J. Smith, which the Museum now holds. Another valued source of photographs was the Sid Nash collection in the hands of the Stephenson Locomotive Society. Gerry Nichols, SLS librarian, also took much time and effort in response to my requests and queries, without which the pages that follow would have been all the poorer. I should also mention Hugh Davies, another SLS member who also runs the 'Photographs from the Fifties' archive. Not intending to appear lazy, but the response to my, 'What have you got on the Cuckoo Line...?' was dealt with promptly and efficiently. Gentlemen, thank you.

A number of individuals have also assisted with images, including Terry Cole, Jeffery Grayer, Trevor Owen, Roger Holmes and David Wallis.

I must include David Vaughan. A brief mention of the project to him produced the totally unexpected, 'I think I know someone who worked on the Cuckoo Line – would you like me to speak to him for you...?' This was at a time when a few personal health issues precluded much travel, so I am grateful to David for his efforts on my behalf. But that was not all, for it transpired it was not just one former railwayman but three who became involved: Richard ('Dick') Brown, Keith Holland, and Roy Townsend. Gentlemen, thank you too. More of their stories relative to areas other than the Cuckoo Line will appear in *Southern Way* in due course.

Finally, thanks to Christopher Fifield for his painstaking advice as to where things could be improved!

The following sources and records have been consulted:

The Cuckoo Line by Alan Elliot, published by Wild Swan. A truly excellent book containing much detail.

Branch Lines around Tunbridge Wells by Vic Mitchell and Keith Smith, published by Middleton Press

The Railways of Mid-Sussex by Adrian Gray, published by Oakwood Press

The London, Brighton & South Coast Railway, Part 3, by J. T. Howard-Turner, published by Batsford

Locomotives of the LBSCR, Parts 1-3m by D. L. Bradley, published by the RCTS

The Hellingly Hospital Railway by Peter Harding, privately published by the author

An Illustrated History of Southern Pull-Push Stock by Mike King, published by OPC

Industrial Railways and Locomotives of Sussex and Surrey compiled by Frank Jux and Roger Hateley, published by the Industrial Railway Society

The Railway Magazine for February 1969: article by H. R. Stones

The Railway Observer, in particular September 1949 and August 1965

The records and drawings of the Signalling Record Society have also been consulted, including, *LBSCR Signal Boxes 1920-1922, Part 2: East of the London and Brighton Line* by J. M. Wagstaff

Railways – various issues

The Southern Railway Magazine – various issues

The Cuckoo Line
A potted history

In attempting to describe the final years of the Cuckoo line in rural Sussex, it is first necessary to turn the clock back more than 160 years, to the year 1849, to 14 May to be precise, the date when the first section of what was officially then the Polegate and Hailsham branch opened.

In our 21st-century world we cannot imagine the effect the new railways were having upon the population as a whole. In general terms, the new mode of transport was opening up the countryside like never before, providing opportunities for the transport of goods, produce and passengers in a form and at a speed that could never have been imagined only a decade or two earlier. In the earliest days, what railways there were had been conceived purely for the transport of goods, usually coal, from pit to port or pit to customer. Likewise the earliest railways were based around the North of England and, even if the inhabitants of rural Sussex had learned of their development, it is hard to imagine that they thought a railway might one day come to them. Possibly the nearest comparison we might make today is the internet compared with letter post. At first email was the province of a few and considered unlikely to have any major impact upon communication, yet within a decade there are now more who do have access than who do not.

No doubt the good folk of Hailsham and Polegate both hoped for and expected great things from their new railway. After all, it was part of a major company, the London, Brighton & South Coast Railway, which on the same date as the opening to Hailsham had opened a second branch south of Polegate to reach Eastbourne. This coastal town features only marginally in what follows, although the opportunity cannot be missed to repeat how such places were often described in Victorian times as 'watering holes', no doubt an accepted phrase in use up to and including the early years of the 20th century but otherwise one that is consigned to the pages of this and other works attempting to capture the atmosphere of the time.

Unfortunately the celebrations of the opening day were marred by a fatal accident, the victim being a young railwayman by the name of John Hield, son of the Bexhill station master and normally employed by the LBSCR as a ticket collector at Brighton. For this special day he had been elevated to the temporary role of passenger guard and was thus occupied in what was a 'guard's box' atop the carriage on one of the celebratory services running south from Hailsham towards Polegate.

For reasons that are not reported, he got down from his guard's box while the train was in motion with the intention of speaking to a passenger. In the days before the advent of corridors, he could only do this by standing on the carriage step, and it was while so occupied that he evidently failed to notice the approach of Mulbrook (Molebrook – sic) level crossing about half a mile south of Hailsham. The impact of human body against solid structure (we are not told what, but it matters not) could only have one result. Poor John was dead before he could be attended to by a doctor.

Tragedy apart, the new railway quickly settled down to provide a regular service, even if in those earliest days the method of timetabling might appear today as almost farcical. This came about because the LBSCR company had allocated just two steam engines for the service from Polegate to Eastbourne and Polegate to Hailsham. Both were stationed at Eastbourne, although only one was used at a time. It should also be noted that both the Eastbourne and Hailsham branches arrived at Polegate from the east – that is facing towards Brighton – so through running between Eastbourne and Hailsham was not possible without a reversal at Polegate. In practice the Eastbourne train would arrive at Polegate and disgorge its passengers. The engine would then take the train to Hailsham, returning from there to Polegate whereupon it became its turn to take a train south again to Eastbourne. Passengers arriving at Polegate, seeing the train arrive from north or south and reasonably expecting the service to return again in the near future, were thus sadly disappointed, finding little comfort from watching the train steam away in the opposite direction.

Quite how long this debacle continued is not certain, and in reality is of little consequence. Suffice to say that just five years later, in 1854, there were nine trains in each direction between Polegate and Hailsham, the last service departing from what was then the terminus at Hailsham at 10.30pm, ironically the same hour of the day that the very last passenger service would leave Hailsham when the railway closed in 1968.

We now need to discuss railway development further north, which in turn would eventually lead to expansion from Hailsham. At the northern end of what would eventually become the Cuckoo Line, a separate railway had opened from Groombridge to Uckfield on 3 August 1868, the route being extended south to Lewes in October of the same year. Before then, the gaps were ready to be filled when the Brighton, Uckfield & Tunbridge Wells Company was incorporated in 1861, followed by the East Grinstead, Groombridge & Tunbridge Wells Company in 1862. The line from Three Bridges to Tunbridge Wells (via East Grinstead High Level and Groombridge) opened on 1 October 1866, with the connecting line from Uckfield via Eridge opening on 3 August 1868. The final part of the route opened on 1 February 1876, a connection between the LBSCR station at Tunbridge Wells West and Tunbridge Wells Central, the station operated by the South Eastern Railway (SER). This single-line section passed through the short Grove Tunnel to Grove Junction, sited a little south of the SER station on its Hastings line.

Meanwhile the SER, the Brighton's rival, was known to have its eyes on developing its own system in the area, and in an attempt to thwart any such encroachment the LBSCR promoted a line from Tunbridge Wells to Eastbourne, the lower half of which would form an end-on connection with the existing terminus at Hailsham.

Today it might seem strange that such inter-company or inter-area rivalry should exist, but we should not forget that this was still an age in which railways were being promoted in their tens, if not hundreds, throughout the country, and it was often a case of 'first past the post' when it came to securing approval by Parliament for a proposal, which would then effectively prohibit any form of competitive plan being sanctioned. Parliament was unlikely to agree to duplicate lines being promoted by differing concerns, especially in the same geographical area. This resulted in the veritable mishmash we have today, the early railways being laid out to suit contemporary needs, and the 20th and 21st centuries having to fit around them.

It might therefore seem that the LBSCR had scored a victory over its rival, but matters would turn as a result of the financial crisis of 1866, in consequence of which proposed work on the route from Tunbridge Wells to Hailsham was halted, although at this stage no actual land work had been started.

There matters rested until 1873, when a nominally independent concern revived the idea for a connection between the two localities, but whose projections were now based on local traffic alone. In consequence the railway was laid out to follow a curved route intended to serve as many towns as possible over its length, but which resulted in a number of severe gradients and sharp curves. One interesting aspect of the 1873 proposal was that the new line to Hailsham should be at a gauge of just 3 feet – fortunately this later changed to standard gauge.

The new proposal had the backing of the South Eastern Railway, which had its eyes on the prize of Eastbourne. To prevent the SER gaining a share of what would be lucrative traffic, the LBSCR was left with little option but to take over the concern in return for a payment of £8,534. In addition there was a concession that receipts from Eastbourne would be pooled between the LBSCR and SER. This was not such a bad idea for either party: for its part, the SER got a share of traffic for no effort, and for the LBSCR it kept a rival out of 'its' territory on terms that could have been a lot worse. The LBSCR had recently gained a similar advantage in the form of a pooling arrangement further west along the coast at Portsmouth, although in this case the other party was the London & South Western Railway.

North of Hailsham, the new line would be single track with passing loops at each station except Hellingly, and would connect end-on with the existing branch at Hailsham. At the north end, it would run parallel with the Uckfield line over the last 1¾ miles to Eridge. The new railway was opened in stages, Hailsham to Heathfield on 5 April 1880, then Heathfield to Eridge on 1 September 1880. The contractor responsible for the line north of Hailsham was Messrs J. T. Chappell.

Meanwhile, at Polegate the inconvenience of having the line from Hailsham arriving at the station facing west was becoming an inconvenience and likely to be ever more so once the 'Heathfield line' was a through route. Consequently the last section south from Hailsham was diverted to face east and run into a new station at Polegate with effect from 3 October 1881. At the same time alterations were made to the line south from Polegate to Eastbourne, resulting in through running without the need to change direction (or train) at Polegate.

Further development occurred in 1894 when the point of convergence of the Heathfield line with that from Uckfield became a proper junction when the Oxted line was doubled. The new location was given the name Redgate Mill Junction, and it was from this point that the Cuckoo Line proper was said to start.

Any subsequent railway development in the area would be mainly confined to what was a new spur north of Eridge (doubled in 1914), which allowed for through running between London and the Uckfield/Heathfield lines without the need to turn east to Groombridge/Tunbridge Wells and the ensuing reversal of directions. Indeed, for a time there were through carriages from London for Eastbourne routed over the Cuckoo Line, detached initially at Groombridge and later Eridge.

Through traffic of sorts would continue throughout the life of the line, but through trains were not the mainstay of services, these instead being restricted to local trains operating from Tunbridge Wells West to Eastbourne, or 'short workings' primarily from the southern end terminating at either Hailsham or Heathfield before working back whence they had come. This would continue to be the pattern of services for the next 80 years until the social upheaval of the mid-20th century, followed by a move away from the railway as the principal means of transport towards the bus and private motor car.

It could not therefore have come as any real surprise when, in response to falling receipts, consideration for closure in stages was announced, culminating in the last passenger train leaving Hailsham for Polegate at 10.30pm on 8 September 1968.

While the usual protestations had been heard, it was a common if not ironic feature of the raft of closures of the 1960s that the hundreds who would turn out to witness such events and mourn the passing of 'their railway' were not so willing to use it on a regular basis and so perhaps contribute towards its continued survival.

That said, the policy of the railways in the 1960s was very much based around the politics of the time and, as with anything, whether it be the attitudes of the time, tastes, fashion, or even local railways, it is difficult if not dangerous to attempt comparisons with the present situation half a century later. Yes, there were some BR managers who fought for closures, encouraged to do so and indeed rewarded for the amount of money they could save. Others strove to retain services, often in the hope that the public attitude and political climate might change, governments of the time being voted into office on a policy of 'no more rail closures', then proceeding to renege on such a policy as soon as they were safely installed in power. It was corruption in all but name.

Regarding the political situation, it should not be forgotten that the railways were not at the top of the list when it came to investment. In order to achieve modernisation, sacrifices had to be made, even if – and here we speak in general rather than in any specific terms – figures were sometimes 'manipulated' or traffic deliberately discouraged through timetable changes that left long periods without trains or, worse, deliberately contrived missed connections.

Generally what the railways had been left with in the 1960s was either the traffic no one else wanted or which was difficult to place elsewhere. This included commuter traffic (where there was and still is no real alternative) and (on the freight side) coal, for most homes were without central heating and coal was still the fuel of necessity. Thus even when a railway closed, the goods yard might remain open for coal traffic, as would prove to be the case with the Cuckoo Line.

It should also be said (as we shall see in the illustrations that follow) that economy and money-saving were certainly not words restricted to the 1960s. They had applied even a century before, when the LBSCR had cancelled work in progress on various lines due to the prevailing economic situation. Later, the company would economise operations by closing unnecessary or superseded facilities – the engine shed at Hailsham, for example. Its successor, the Southern Railway, proceeded in similar fashion, economising the signalling at several of the Cuckoo Line stations but, as mentioned, it was British Railways under the stewardship of Dr Beeching that would create the greatest change, and not in the form of restricted facilities – but rather no facilities at all!

In the 21st century some extant signs of what had once been a prosperous railway are still to be found, principally in the 14 miles of 'The Cuckoo Trail' south from Heathfield through Horam, Hailsham and Polegate, and continuing on to Eastbourne. Elsewhere residential, road or industrial development might have replaced the trains, but despite these best efforts there is still plenty to see of the efforts of the railway builders, together with the employment and transport links the railway once provided. Structures and earthworks may not always be immediately obvious, but they are still there if time is spent searching them out.

Why 'Cuckoo'?

At first glance the reference to the 'Cuckoo Line' might appear to refer to the migratory bird and its unique call. Was the line named after this dove-sized bird renowned for taking over a nest prepared and made ready by another? The short answer is an emphatic 'No'.

In itself this might appear surprising, for locally certain lines (branch-type routes in particular) have long been referenced by a specific word. The 'Bluebell' line is arguably the most famous, but others include 'Strawberry', 'Lavender', 'Abbey', etc.

Having established that it has absolutely nothing to do with hearing the bird while travelling along the railway, we need to dig slightly deeper into the origins of the name, and these are not difficult to find. The answer could not be more straightforward. It takes its name from the 'Cuckoo Fair' held annually at Heathfield, usually around 14 April, where a cuckoo was released from a basket to denote the arrival of spring. Originally a livestock and produce market, the Cuckoo Fair has in more recent times morphed into what we would now recognise as a county show, while the release of an actual cuckoo (usually more than one) still takes place.

With the railway serving Heathfield, it was a small step for the line to become known as the 'Cuckoo Line', certainly within the locality, then by both staff and passengers alike. Legend has it that the name was first used by the navvies building the route and was thus passed on to the first railwaymen. To staff some distance away, and most certainly those ensconced in the offices at Waterloo or wherever, the more official description was the 'Heathfield line'. In an attempt to strike a balance we will mix and match the terms in the pages that follow; and unless stated otherwise, the descriptions that follow are applicable to how the railway would have been seen in the British Railways era.

Tunbridge Wells West

Tunbridge Wells West (TWW) station was the terminus for most passenger trains operating between Tunbridge Wells and Eastbourne. While historically the line may have been opened in a south-to-north direction, we will look at it from the opposite perspective of north to south, starting here. Geographically placed in an east-west position, there were up and down platforms with the main station building on the north (down) side of the site. The platform on the south (up) side was an island, allowing trains to the Cuckoo Line and those to Lewes via Uckfield, East Grinstead and Oxted to have the use of either of the two platform faces. To the east, the line became single before passing through the 183-yard Grove Tunnel to join the SER route from Hastings to Tonbridge at Grove Junction, just south of the other station that served the town, Tunbridge Wells Central. Goods and siding facilities were provided at the West station, together with a four-road engine shed, coded 75F from 1950 until 1963, then, as depots closed and steam working was consolidated at fewer points, 75A from 1963 until 1965, and finally 75C in 1965. The parent depot responsible during that period was variously Redhill or Brighton, which were respectively 75B and 75A. A 46-foot turntable was provided at the western end of the shed site, no doubt perfectly suitable for all engine types in the early days; however, as machines grew larger in later years it was only the smallest tender engines together with various tank engine types that could make use of it. The turntable was removed around 1961, but the shed continued in use.

Before the Second World War various small former Brighton tanks had found a home here, being responsible for working trains to Victoria, over the Oxted line, to East Grinstead and of course Cuckoo Line workings. As these were slowly withdrawn, they were replaced by the LBSCR 4-4-2T types ('I1X' and 'I3') and the two large LBSCR ('Baltic') 4-6-2 tanks (Classes 'J1' and 'J2' respectively), also working trains from the depot. In turn, both types were replaced in BR days by modern steam in the form of first Fairburn then BR Standard Class 4MT locos – not without too much in the way of nostalgia from the crews, we can be sure.

This is the view looking west through Tunbridge Wells West station towards Groombridge and (with a bit of poetic licence) the Cuckoo Line. The main buildings are on the right-hand side, the engine shed hidden beyond these and on the left a glimpse of the commodious goods shed. Recorded towards the end of the life of the station, the yard is conspicuously devoid of goods traffic, while the engine release crossover, no longer needed for the final years of DEMU operation, has been rendered out of use. Modern BR electric lighting is visible but, apart from one pedestrian, part hidden on the right, the station is devoid of life. *Martin Dean*

Looking east from the end of the platform on 12 June 1965, the appropriately named 'East' signal box is visible. The single-bore Grove Tunnel may also be seen. *J. J. Smith, courtesy Bluebell Railway Museum*

Signal box diagram, Tunbridge Wells West.

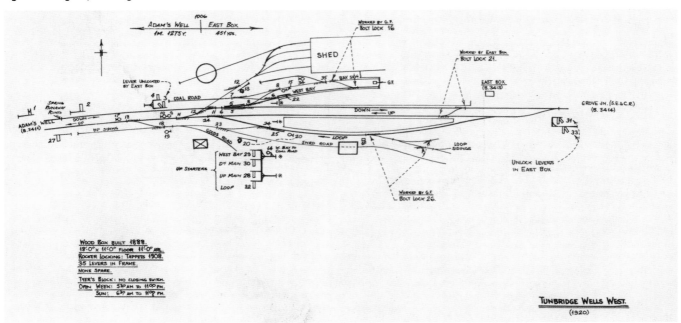

'H' Class 0-4-4T No 31519 stands in the bay at the eastern end of Platform 2 on 21 February 1960. This would likely be a pull-push working. *Hugh Davies, 'Photos from the Fifties'*

Still retaining signs of Southern Railway ownership, 'E4' Class 0-6-2T No (3)2581 waits in steam outside the front of the shed in 1949. Tunbridge Wells and area was where any amount of variety in steam types might be seen, with examples of former SECR, LBSCR, LSWR, SR, LMSR and BR designs working hand-in-hand, approximately 20 steam engines being allocated here in the post-war period. This particular machine was a long-term resident of the shed and was withdrawn from here at the end of April 1962. *S. C. Nash, Stephenson Locomotive Society collection*

The enemy visited the railway at Tunbridge Wells on 20 November 1940, at least one bomb passing through the shed roof. Apart from those engines allocated for duty at the depot, the shed was also host to several stored locos, the practice being to spread resources around the railway. Two members of the 'I3' Class were stored here at the time, Nos 2021 and 2024, together with others of similar type as part of the operational allocation. It appears that the bomb passed through the shed roof, exploding in the arches beneath the track with sufficient force to derail at least one engine (No 2007). In this series of views workmen are seen inspecting the damage. Details of any casualties or other incidents affecting the railway in the area at this time are not reported. *All Southern Railway, Jeremy Cobb collection*

An unfortunate incident involving Stroudley 'C1' Class 0-6-0 goods engine No 423 on the turntable at Tunbridge Wells West occurred on 11 March 1905. How it came to be driven into the open pit will doubtless remain a mystery, although packing is already in place as part of the recovery operation to come. The leading axle of the tender has also been supported, allowing pressure to be reduced on the engine-to-tender drawbar that, once disconnected, will allow the engine to be recovered.

Spare coaching stock comprising former SECR 'birdcage' vehicles stands in the siding alongside the island platform on 21 February 1960. *Hugh Davies, 'Photos from the Fifties'*

Below: Ancient and modern: on the left is 'I1X' 4-4-2T No 32002 and on the right the modern replacement of Fairburn 2-6-4T No 42098. The view was taken in 1951, with the 'I1X' not long for this world, being withdrawn on the last day of July, exactly 44 years to the day since its construction. *S. C. Nash, Stephenson Locomotive Society collection*

This is one of the big 4-6-2T engines that also ended their days on local trains in the area. The type had been barred from the line for many years, but this prohibition was relaxed from April 1944. Seen here is unique 'J1' Class No 32325 still in Southern green livery, built in 1910, still active in 1950 but taken out of use in the summer of 1951. The headcode indicates an Eastbourne train, while the loco duty, in this case No 666, has been affixed to the disc. The 'birdcage' lookout is also visible on the coach set. One wonders how much coal might be accidentally lost en route! *E. R. Wethersett*

Freight at Tunbridge Wells West: one of the ubiquitous 'C2X' 0-6-0 tender engines, No 32434, is recorded in the yard in 1950 on what appears to be a limited revenue freight – or possibly shunting duties. The engine has been fitted with a double-domed boiler and would be active for 64 years, being withdrawn from traffic in 1957. *S. C. Nash, Stephenson Locomotive Society collection*

Opposite: As proof of the variety of engines working trains into, through and from Tunbridge Wells West in the 1950s, here is a former SECR 'D' Class 4-4-0, now BR No 31549, departing from the station westbound and displaying the headcode for a Cuckoo Line train. The front of the engine shed is to the left. *S. C. Nash, Stephenson Locomotive Society collection*

Cuckoo Line Memories 1
Keith Holland

Interviewed by David Vaughan

DV: 'How and when did you start working on the railways?'

KH: 'I was always interested in the railway and my cousin was a fireman at Tunbridge Wells West shed (code 75F) so I asked him if he would ask the shed master, Mr Charlie Stone, if there were any vacancies for cleaners. I was told to write to Mr Stone stating my interest. I received a reply from him that a medical had been arranged for me with a doctor at Brighton Works; the letter contained a free travel pass. I passed the medical and went to see Mr Stone with a letter from the doctor confirming this. I left school on 18 December 1953 at the age of 15 and the very next day reported to the shed foreman at 8am as a cleaner.'

DV: 'How did you get on?'

KH: 'On becoming 16 I became a passed cleaner and covered for firemen; this was mainly on shed duties, preparing and disposing engines and moving them around the shed roads.'

DV: 'So when did you become a loco fireman?'

KH: 'Late in 1954 I was rostered as a fireman. There were three links at Tunbridge Wells West. I was rostered into Link 3 and worked on many duties, both goods and passenger trains, but it was not until eight years later, in 1962, when I became a passed fireman, that I was allowed onto driving duties.'

DV: 'What do you remember of your early days as a fireman?'

KH: 'One of the first duties I had was on a regular run from Tunbridge Wells to Three Bridges [not a Cuckoo Line service] with a goods train. This set off at 2pm and stopped all the way – Withyham, Hartfield, Forest Row, Rowfant – before arriving at Three Bridges. At each of the intermediate stations we would shunt wagons off and pick up others as necessary. One trip I remember in particular, we were on an "E4" radial – we had two of these at "the Wells", Nos 2581 and 82 [locomen still referred to these engines by their former SR numbers despite a "3" prefix having been added by BR in 1948]. I did not know the driver but when he got on board he put a sort of case on the ledge on the back box. As we got near Rowfant, the driver, who of course had been keeping a sharp lookout, said, "Right boy, this is where you lose your hat...". To my surprise he opened up the case and took out a shotgun. He then leaned out of the cab, took aim and shot a passing pheasant. With that he grabbed my hat and threw it out near to where the dead bird had landed. The return duty was with a passenger service and before we left I recall the driver saying to the guard, "On the way back we will be struggling a bit on the bank up to Rowfant but don't worry about it." So we crawled up the bank and when the driver spotted my hat he stopped the train, got down, recovered the pheasant and also my hat!

The Eastbourne goods [via the Cuckoo Line] was worked by a 'C' Class [ex-SECR] with an Eastbourne crew, so the only goods work we had was from Tunbridge Wells to Three Bridges. I enjoyed the run with a passenger train from "the Wells" to Brighton. We used to go down, often with an "L" Class 4-4-0 or an "N" Class "Mogul". Later on we had Standard Class 4s. We would go on to the top turntable [at Brighton], turn and take water and then come back again and that was all of our 8-hour shift. Once you

Keith Holland is the driver in the cab of Redhill-based BR Class 4 'Mogul' No 76061 at Eastbourne, having just arrived with a train off the Cuckoo Line. *Keith Holland*

left Crowborough, it was an easy run all downhill to Lewes, but then of course we had Falmer bank to climb before we got to Brighton. The "L" Class had big driving wheels and really galloped along nicely. The bank up from Eridge to Crowborough presented no problem to them.'

DV: 'You mentioned that there were three links at Tunbridge Wells West – which ones were you allocated to?'

KH: 'Well, eventually I worked through all of them but to start with I was in Link 3, which worked trains on the lines to Three Bridges, Brighton, Lewes and of course the Cuckoo Line. Before the Bluebell Line was closed by British Railways, we also worked a train from East Grinstead to Lewes, normally with an Ivatt 2 or a Standard 4 tank.

The second link worked mainly push-pull trains from Tunbridge Wells to Oxted, originally with "H" Class tanks. Later we had "M7s" and, after that, Ivatt Class 2 tanks, but they were not fitted with push-pull equipment. We also did one early-morning trip to Uckfield and then back up to Oxted.'

DV: 'What were the engines on the push-pull service like to handle?'

KH: 'Well, we had some fun when we first got the "M7s". The "H" Class liked a fire built up to the back door of the firebox and then let it drift down towards the front, but the "M7s" liked a flat fire built up in the back corners. They were prone to priming if you had too much water, so you made sure you ran with half a glass showing in the gauge glass. I think they were more powerful than the "H" Class tanks. One of the fireman's duties of course was to keep an eye on the water level and use the injectors to top it up when needed. Intelligent use of the injectors, which could often be troublesome to operate, was vital to the good steaming of a locomotive. Too much water when going downhill could cause priming, while too little water going uphill could spell disaster!'

DV: 'So when you moved up to the first link, what duties did you have then?'

KH: 'That was the main-line passenger run from Tunbridge Wells to London Victoria or London Bridge via East Grinstead or Edenbridge. That train usually had eight coaches but they later increased it to nine. We couldn't keep nine coaches at the Wells, so we had to run light engine out to Groombridge, where there was a longer siding, and then bring the train back empty stock before we started. I well remember the 7.12am train to Victoria because that was the train where I met my wife, who used it to travel up to London to work each day.'

DV: 'What engines were used on the London runs?'

KH: 'We either had a Standard 4 tank or a Fairburn. In my opinion the Fairburn

2-6-4 tanks were the more powerful of the two, although of course they were a similar design. They were good, hard-working engines.'

DV: 'Can you tell me about your experience of driving or firing on the Cuckoo Line?'

KH: 'Most of the trips I did on that line were in the third or second link and all on passenger trains, for, as I mentioned earlier, the Eastbourne crew did the pick-up goods. On one of the late-evening trips we did pick up a milk tank from the Express Dairy at Horam and dropped it off at Groombridge for onward journey to London with a passenger train. We had one top-link turn, which involved going down the Cuckoo Line to Eastbourne, sometimes with a Standard Class 4 tank engine, a type I liked very much. We would go to the shed for water, turn and then pick up the holiday train that was known as "The Birkenhead Flyer" (officially "The Sunny South Special") and go to Brighton via Lewes with it, drop it off in the station, run-round, go to the top turntable, turn and water, then work back to Tunbridge Wells.' [See the photo on page 104].

Fairburn tank No 42104 has arrived at Tunbridge Wells West with a train off the Cuckoo Line. *Keith Holland*

DV: 'What were your memories of the Cuckoo Line?'

KH: 'Well, it was an interesting line because it was either uphill or down dale, wherever you went. Coming from Tunbridge Wells to Eridge and then Redgate Mill Junction, where you picked up the staff for the next section, was all right, after that it was all uphill to Rotherfield. Then uphill again to Argos Hill Tunnel, then you dropped down to Mayfield. At Mayfield there was a very sharp curve where you had to be careful with your speed, because years ago a train derailed there and went out in the field. [The ruling or line speed was only 25mph.] After that, you came out of a dip and it was a long climb up to Heathfield. The rest was easy, downhill or flat all the way to Eastbourne. Coming back, it was a long steep climb from Horam to Heathfield, which of course took the steam out of our sails. As a fireman, it was hard work and you had to keep on top of it. I remember that on the way up from Hellingly to Horam there was a farm that lay over the bank and two farm girls lived there. They used to come out regularly and wave to us and at Christmas time put up a banner that said "Happy Christmas loco-men". Years later I got a job on Parcel Force and had a delivery to that farm. I spoke to the lady living there and asked if she had two daughters. Well, it wasn't her but she said she knew who they were and that they were both out in Australia. Once we had slogged up to Heathfield we had to take water, especially if we had a small engine. At Hailsham, Heathfield, Mayfield and Rotherfield there was also the staff to collect from the signalman ready for the next section. I once had a bet with an Eastbourne engineman, who reckoned that we couldn't do a complete trip from Eastbourne to Tunbridge Wells West on one firebox full of coal. Well we did!'

DV: 'How did you manage that?'

KH: 'Well, we filled the box right up to the backhead and stacked a few lumps of coal round the cab, just in case. This was on a Standard 4 2-6-4 tank, which was a nice easy-going engine and a good steamer. Now, the last trip back from Eastbourne arrived at the sheds [Tunbridge Wells West] at 9.30pm and the Cornwallis pub shut at 10pm on a weekday. My driver and I were a good team and so we arranged that when we arrived back at the shed, there was only the bare minimum of fire left. We turned, watered the engine ready for the next day's duty and disposed of the fire – the Standard 4s had a rocking grate so it was easy – and we still managed to get time for a couple of pints!'

DV: 'What engines did you have experience on over the Cuckoo Line?'

KH: 'There was quite a varied selection. Our shed fielded "H" Class and "M7" tanks, as well as Standard 4 and Fairburn 2-6-4 tanks, and then there were "E4s" and Ivatt 2-6-2 tanks, not forgetting the Standard 4 tender engines. These only worked one way from Eastbourne to Tunbridge Wells with a Tunbridge Wells crew and then onward to Redhill by a Tonbridge crew.'

DV: 'Did the "West Country" or "Battle of Britain" "light Pacifics" often work on the Cuckoo Line?'

KH: 'I personally did not have any experience of that, but I believe the Brighton crews often worked the odd Bulleid "Pacific" on a fill-in turn from Eastbourne as far as Hailsham or Heathfield. It was all a question of availability.'

DV: 'Did you ever have occasion to work on Bulleid's "Q1" Class on the Cuckoo Line?'

KH: 'They did sometimes work on that route but the only time I remember crewing one was from Victoria on a passenger.'

DV: 'Surely that was an unusual loco for that sort of working? How did it come about?'

KH. 'That was because we dropped the brick arch on the Standard tank we went up on. It was not a common occurrence of course, but with a lot of hard working the arch could become brittle after a time and sometimes, without warning, that did happen. Anyway, we phoned Stewarts Lane and asked for a spare engine. They said, "We're short of engines but we'll see what we can do." They sent over a "Q1". We only had five or six bogies on, so it had no trouble with that, but going through Clapham Junction you had to hold on because they really rocked and rolled, did the old "Q1s".'

In the freezing winter of 1963, 'Q' Class No 30543 takes water at Tunbridge Wells West. In conditions such as these, it was not unknown for the water column to freeze – despite the efforts of a fire in a brazier underneath, specifically intended to prevent this from happening. *Keith Holland*

BR Standard tank No 80149 being turned at Tunbridge Wells West. The turntable was hand-operated! This and the 'Q' Class were the largest class of engine that could use the turntable. *Keith Holland*

DV: 'I imagine by this time steam was on the way out, so I understand you finished up on the DEMUs known as "Thumpers"?'

KH: 'Yes that's right. We had to go to Stewarts Lane for a week's training in the classroom, the basic stuff, and then we went to Ashford for three days practical with an instructor on the Ashford to Hastings line, where they were already regularly working. First time out it was a bit frightening, as I was used to the vacuum braking system, putting it on when you first see the station. However, going into Appledore station the instructor said, "Don't touch that brake!" and I thought we shall never stop. Then he said, "Full application, hold it and then gradually release it as you come up the platform and you'll stop just right." As I found out, that was a feature of the EPS [Electro-Pneumatic System] braking system and I thought, well this is all right.'

DV: 'So what were the diesels like on the old Cuckoo Line? I suppose, after the steam engines, they were a lot easier to handle?'

KH: 'Well yes, they were, but with a line speed of just 25mph you had to wait at each station to make up time or you quickly got ahead of yourself.'

DV: 'They were certainly quite nippy, but I had a cab ride in one and I remember they were pretty noisy.'

The modern replacement for the steam services: 'Sussex' DEMU unit No 1309 arrives at Tunbridge Wells West forming the 9.45am Eastbourne to Tonbridge service via the Cuckoo Line on 7 July 1962. The headcode '31' was given for these workings. For the final year or so of operation, the DEMUs were replaced by steam. *D. S. Pollard*

KH: 'Yes, they were a bit noisy, especially on the Horam to Heathfield bank when you had to open them up. It was a much easier life driving the diesels but I did enjoy my time on the footplate of a steam engine.'

Keith left the railway in 1965 and had a number of different jobs before finally retiring in 2005. But steam men never really retire, and Keith can often be found as a crew member aboard *Wilbur*, a 20-ton, 1917-built Fowler ploughing engine with his friend Brian Tompsett on the road to a Sussex steam engine rally. He is also a volunteer fireman on the Spa Valley Railway, which operates from his old stamping ground at Tunbridge Wells West and runs as far as Eridge, over the line on which he once worked BR steam engines.

Groombridge

West from Tunbridge Wells West, the railway passed High Rocks Halt and the small level crossing at Adam's Well to reach Groombridge, just over 2 miles 61 chains from departure, distances being measured between signal boxes. This is a view of the station looking east in March 1948 with a subway in use connecting the platforms. *LGRP*

Signal box diagram, Groombridge East.

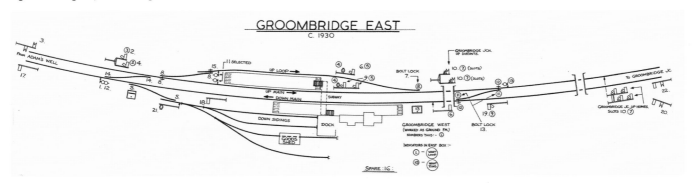

On a wet 22 December 1962 'H' Class 0-4-4T No 31551 arrives at the staggered platforms en route to Tunbridge Wells West.
Hugh Davies, 'Photos from the Fifties'

With a number of obvious steam leaks, 'I3' 4-4-2T No 32075 was another former Brighton engine not long for this world. It is seen at Groombridge, but would succumb at the end of October 1951. *S. C. Nash, Stephenson Locomotive Society collection*

Busy times in 1951: No 32030 is on a Cuckoo Line train heading towards Tunbridge Wells West, while waiting in the yard is 'N' Class 'Mogul' No 31412. *S. C. Nash, Stephenson Locomotive Society collection*

Groombridge Junction

Leaving Groombridge, the railway turned south, taking the left fork at Groombridge Junction, less than a mile from the station from which it took its name. Taking the right fork, the line continued west towards East Grinstead or north to Oxted. The route was now south, with a trailing entry at Birchden Junction to head towards Eridge.

The signalman's perspective at Groombridge Junction, looking north-east, with the line from Ashurst Junction in the left foreground (East Grinstead and Oxted), while that on the right is from Birchden Junction (Uckfield and the Cuckoo Line). Photographed on 14 April 1923 by Edward Wallis, the signals are set for a train to take the south to north-west route towards Groombridge and Tunbridge Wells. *David Wallis*

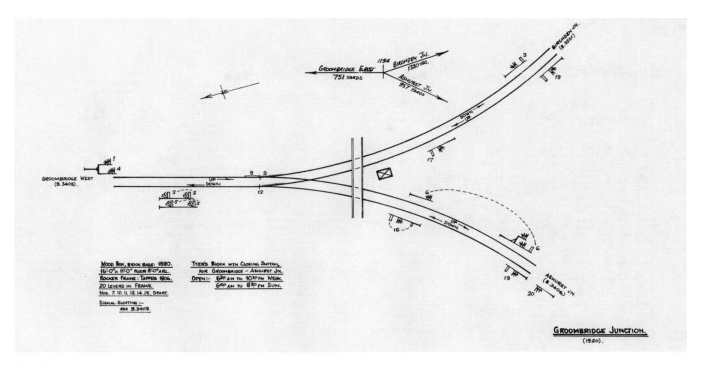

Signal box diagram, Groombridge Junction

On the same date we look south-west from the direction of Groombridge station towards the junction. The signal box is in the 'V' of the two routes preceded by what was known as the upside-down footbridge. The junction signal had elevated co-acting arms that provided advance warning to drivers of the route set and signal position, and were a common feature throughout the railways until well into the 20th century. *David Wallis*

Eridge

At the south end of what was in effect a triangle of lines, Cuckoo Line services would join the chord from Ashurst Junction at Birchden Junction before arrival at Eridge. Here had been the original point of convergence for Uckfield and Cuckoo Line trains until the former route was doubled in 1894. The main station building was located on the bridge that carried the A26 road over the railway at the south end. Originally provided with just a single platform serving the then single line, the facilities were extended in 1880 to provide two island platforms together with the usual goods facilities. In this view, looking south, BR 4MT 2-6-4T No 80084 leaves from the up loop with the 12.40pm Eastbourne to Tunbridge Wells West working on a wet 21 March 1964. In the background is a DEMU service from the Uckfield line. The allocation of the BR 4MT tank engines was intended to improve reliability and punctuality of train working in the Sussex area, and to a great extend this was achieved. Even so, schedules were still slow in the main, although an attempt was made in 1956 with a regular-interval timetable providing an hourly service over the Cuckoo Line. At Waterloo it was hoped that such moves would placate 'Disgusted of Tunbridge Wells', the colloquial name given to the persistent complainer originating from middle England. *Hugh Davies, 'Photos from the Fifties'*

Signal box diagrams, Eridge North and South.

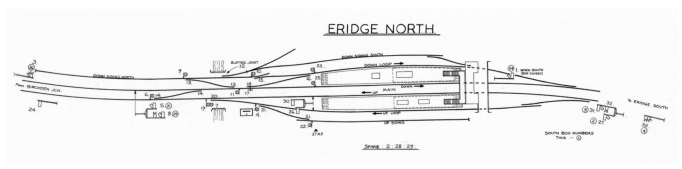

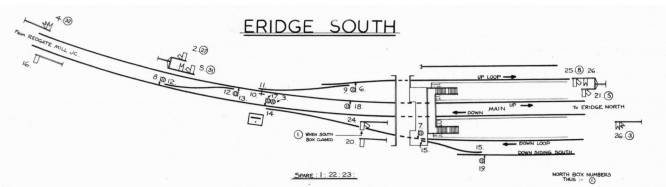

Examples of the variety of motive power that might be seen at the station: the first is former LSWR 'T9' 4-4-0 No (30)304 some miles away from its original haunts, recorded in 1949. *S. C. Nash, Stephenson Locomotive Society collection*

This time it is the turn of a Southern Railway-built 'Q' Class 0-6-0, No 30546, leaving the station on the up line in 1950. The headcode is for a Cuckoo Line service. *S. C. Nash, Stephenson Locomotive Society collection*

Now a Brighton 'Atlantic', No 32425 *Trevose Head*, heads south displaying an Uckfield headcode in 1950. Rather than use headcode discs (lamps were used at night), the Southern Railway and its successor the Southern Region preferred to use a code based on the route the train was intended to take. This certainly assisted station staff and signalmen at diverging junctions, but it also meant that the same code would be used regardless of whether the working was a fast passenger or pick-up goods. *S. C. Nash, Stephenson Locomotive Society collection*

Next a 'D3' 0-4-4T No 32368, which had once carried the name *Newport*. This engine would achieve just under 1.5 million miles in operational service over a life of just under 61 years, which ended in February 1953. *S. C. Nash, Stephenson Locomotive Society collection*

Entering Eridge from the north is 'D1' 4-4-0 No 31502, also on an Uckfield line service. *S. C. Nash, Stephenson Locomotive Society collection*

And finally this 1951 portrayal of 'super-power' features a steam-shrouded Bulleid 'Pacific' No 34038 *Lynton* on what is probably a through Brighton to Victoria via Uckfield train. In the bay platform is a double-headed working off the Cuckoo Line, with 'I3' 4-4-2T No 32023 as the pilot engine. (The engine at the front was always known as the 'pilot', while that attached to the train was referred to as the 'train' engine.) No 32023 spent the day working trains over the Cuckoo Line, and would meet No 34038 again later when on the 4.35pm from Tunbridge Wells West and 3.52pm from Victoria respectively.
S. C. Nash, Stephenson Locomotive Society collection

Eridge signal box is seen in 1950. Originally North and South boxes controlled the layout here, but with effect from 21 September 1930 operations were combined at the former North box, renamed 'Eridge'. From 1930 this box contained a frame of 33 levers. *S. C. Nash, Stephenson Locomotive Society collection*

Redgate Mill Junction and Argos Hill

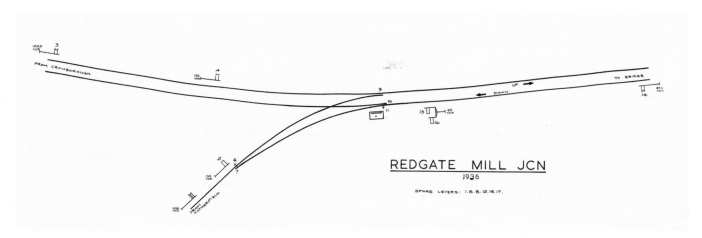

Signal box diagram, Redgate Mill Junction. The name was taken from a nearby farm.

The Cuckoo Line proper began at Redgate Mill Junction, about 1¼ miles from Eridge, and where a signal box on the east side of the line controlled a double-to-single-line junction. In the direction of the first station (Rotherfield & Mark Cross), crews were faced with a stiff climb averaging 1 in 50 as the route took the railway across the Wealdon Ridge, which rises 500 feet above sea level and is also the watershed between the Medway in the north and the Rother in the south. The surrounding area was, and indeed still is, primarily agricultural, so that type of traffic was of great importance in the early years. The climb continued for nearly 2½ miles, near the summit of which was Argos Hill Tunnel. 'I3' 4-4-2T No 32083 is seen in the area of the summit with the 4.39pm Eastbourne to Tunbridge Wells West train on 21 May 1951. *J. J. Smith, courtesy Bluebell Railway Museum*

Another engine working hard on the climb is 'H' Class 0-4-4T No 31328, this time with the 5.55pm Tunbridge Wells West to Eastbourne train on the same day. *J. J. Smith, courtesy Bluebell Railway Museum*

Exemplifying the reverse curvature that was a feature of the route, especially south from the junction as far as Horam, 'I3' 4-4-2T No 32028 is seen with former SECR stock at Argos Hill on 17 July 1951. This is the same working as seen in the previous view, the 5.55pm Tunbridge Wells West to Eastbourne. *J. J. Smith, courtesy Bluebell Railway Museum*

Neat ballast shoulders and cut grass were features of almost every rural railway in the 1950s, typified here as 'C2X' No 32541 heads what is probably the daily pick-up freight at Argos Hill. On average, one of these workings would feature in each direction daily. That doyen of information *The Railway Observer*, in its issue for September 1949, has a correspondent reporting as follows: 'An epidemic of engine failures has brought a remarkable assortment of motive power on to the Heathfield line during recent weeks. The most noteworthy visitant was Drummond "T9" No 304 (BAT), which not only worked the 7.55pm ex-Tunbridge Wells on Bank Holiday, but remained on the service for the two succeeding days, working Eastbourne duty 797. A "Greyhound" on the Cuckoo Line is a rarity indeed. Yet not unheard of, for on a pre-war occasion one of them illicitly worked the 11.08 from Victoria, at a time when the class was prohibited between Hurst Green and Polegate! No 304's appearance was certainly the first legitimate appearance. On the evening of 3 August 1949, the "T9" was replaced by "C2X" 0-6-0 No 32448 (BA), which remained on passenger duties for nearly a week. Also on 3 August, No 2541 (RED) was on the 5.00 Eridge to Eastbourne, while on 15 August No 2554 (BA) essayed some faster work by attempting the 11.08 ex-Victoria, with which she eventually reached Eastbourne, though with considerable time loss. Other strangers to work the 5.00 from Eridge have been "C" 0-6-0s 1102 (BA) and S1513 (TON), also the superheater 4-4-0 No 31165 (BA), the last-named making three consecutive appearances, commencing on 18 July.' Elsewhere the *RO* reports that with the resumption of 'Ramblers Special' workings in the post-war period, the Heathfield line is now being referred to as the 'Cuckoo Line' by British Railways. *S. C. Nash, Stephenson Locomotive Society collection*

In a final view at this location, three-car DEMU No 1308 makes light work of the gradient on 29 February 1964. It was not uncommon to see two three-car diesel sets operating services around this time. This particular diesel unit, together with set No 1303, would, in June 1965, form the last down train over the line, crossing at Rotherfield with set No 1307 heading north.

Following Argos Hill the railway was on a long down gradient for 2¾ miles at 1 in 52/50 passing through a long bridge at a skew under the main road from the south to Tunbridge Wells. This bridge, almost a short tunnel, had no official name and was about halfway down the bank beyond the summit. *J. J. Smith, courtesy Bluebell Railway Museum*

Rotherfield & Mark Cross

Between Redgate Mill Junction and Argos Hill Tunnel was Rotherfield & Mark Cross station. In this early view, the nameboard proclaiming simply 'Rotherfield', we are looking north towards Redgate Mill Junction, with the main buildings on the east, or down, side of the line. As might be expected, there were for many years two signal boxes here, one each at opposite ends of the site. In such cases this was necessary due to the limit then placed on the mechanical operation of points. However, unlike elsewhere on the Cuckoo Line, the two signal boxes were retained throughout the life of the line, albeit that the one at the south end was designated 'NBP', or non-block post. This was necessary as the intention of centralising the lever frame by placing it on the platform was not possible due to the position of the stairwell. Operation of the railway as a single line was initially by 'staff and ticket', but after 1892 Webb-Thompson Electric Train Staff equipment was in use, the instruments for which were located in the former South box. The line north of Hailsham was engineered by Frederick Banister, while the building designs were in the hands of his son-in-law, Thomas Myres. Similar designs by Myres appear at a number of locations, including the stations on the Bluebell Line as well as those at Lavant, Singleton and Cocking. *O. J. Morris*

Frederick D. Banister (1823-97), Engineer of the LBSCR from 1861 to 1895. (https://en.wikipedia.org/wiki/Frederick_Banister)

Below: Signal box diagram, Rotherfield.

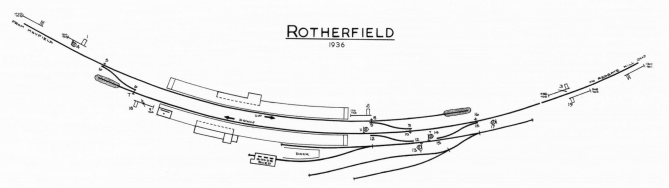

Some decades later, this is the view looking south with the 32-chain (794-yard) curve that ran through the station. The by now faded nameboard proclaims 'Rotherfield and Mark Cross'. As was standard practice on most single lines, trains arriving at the location, regardless of direction, would have a straight run in, only taking a crossover on leaving. The station site was on level ground – useful of course for shunting – although there was a rising 1 in 56 gradient from the north and an even steeper 1 in 50 to the south. A horse box may be seen in the loading bay. The supports for the platform canopy, lamps and running-in board still display wartime stripes, intended to assist passengers in the blackout. The view is probably some time in the 1950s, as concrete sleepers have appeared, although it should be noted that these were still being laid on the line as late as 1964. Note that in the 'four-foot' of the down line (between the rails) a number of derricks have been settled between the sleepers. These were sunk at intervals if it was suspected that 'creep' was occurring, always possible on a curve; the distance between the centre of the derrick and the running rail could then be measured at intervals to assess if movement was taking place. A number of other derricks are scattered in the 'six-foot' (between the two sets of running rails), no doubt ready to be sunk into the up line. *Hugh Davies, 'Photos from the Fifties'*

By 21 March 1964 BR has installed electric lighting, while the derricks referred to above now appear in both lines. BR Standard Class 4MT No 80084 is in charge of the 12.40pm Eastbourne to Tunbridge Wells West – an apparently simple two-coach service. A number of the lamp posts also sport the then standard 'sausage' token in white on green, proclaiming the station name. If only it had been known then that today such pieces of tin would command a figure sometimes in excess of £1,000 each in the hands of collectors! *S. C. Nash, Stephenson Locomotive Society collection*

The (non-block post) signal box at the south end of the station site had an ornate LBSCR design and was likely to have been Myres's work; similar design structures were common throughout the LBSCR. A gradient board is seen together with what is an original LBSCR straight-arm water crane. Unlike at Heathfield, the arm of the water crane is original and was not replaced in later years by one allowing replenishment of locomotive water tanks, which necessitated a design with a higher filling point. A Southern Railway rail-built signal with a corrugated arm acts as the starting signal for the section to Mayfield. *Hugh Davies, 'Photos from the Fifties'*

Unique former LBSCR 'J2' Class 4-6-2T No 32326 departs south from the station in 1950. *S. C. Nash, Stephenson Locomotive Society collection*

In the same year we now see LMS-design 2-6-4T No 42102, seen from the same vantage point. British Railways quickly recognised that the Southern Region was in need of large passenger tank engines – a need never filled after the Sevenoaks disaster of 1927. Those large tank engines that did exist were already considered life-expired, hence the transfer or building of examples of both the Fairburn type and later the BR Standard Class 4 design. *S. C. Nash, Stephenson Locomotive Society collection*

An example of the old order: 'I3' 4-4-2T No 32030 is seen arriving with a down train from Tunbridge Wells West. Station patronage had been reasonable when there was little alterative to the train; however, in best railway tradition the railway was some three-quarters of a mile from the centre of the village it purported to serve and, to make matters worse, 160 feet higher, while Mark Cross was double the distance to the north-east. This was in fact the second station to carry the name 'Rotherfield'; the first had been on the Uckfield line, but was renamed 'Crowborough' a month before the opening of the Cuckoo Line. *S. C. Nash, Stephenson Locomotive Society collection*

In the final years, decidedly unkempt Standard Class 4MT No 80149 waits at the down platform at the head of four Maunsell coaches. *Terry Cole*

Sister engine No 80032 in equally filthy condition has a short Bulleid rake forming its train, waiting to head north around the same time. It may be noted also that the canopy supports have had a lick of paint, a sure sign that a railway was due to close! *Terry Cole*

Diesel replacing steam: 'Hampshire' three-car DEMU set No 1115 forms an Eastbourne to Tunbridge Wells West service, seen departing from the station. From the position of the starting signals, trains appear to be departing or to have departed in both directions. Although unseen here, BR provided enamel boards indicating 'S' and '6' as the point at which the drivers of trains should stop at several of the Cuckoo Line stations. BR had hoped that the introduction of diesel trains would not only attract extra patronage but also reduce operating costs. So far as the former was concerned, this has already been discussed in the Introduction, but as to the latter savings were limited to just one post, namely that of the fireman. *Derek Cross*

In sylvan Sussex countryside near Rotherfield, 'E5' 0-6-2T No 32588 is in charge of a short freight from Tunbridge Wells West to Polegate on 9 February 1952. *J. J. Smith, courtesy Bluebell Railway Museum*

Exactly one week later, the same engine is on the same working, this time with three potential revenue-earning wagons in tow. The small goods yard behind is dominated by coal traffic, the receiving merchants being required to empty the wagons within a specified length of time or pay a 'demurrage' (storage) charge. *J. J. Smith, courtesy Bluebell Railway Museum*

Nearby, 'I3' No 32029 has charge of a mixed Bulleid/Maunsell rake on 22 August 1950 – this same engine was photographed earlier at Groombridge. *J. J. Smith, courtesy Bluebell Railway Museum*

Former SECR 'D' Class 4-4-0 No 31490, proclaiming 'British Railways' somewhere under the grime, leaves the station for Redgate Mill Junction and Tunbridge Wells West on 22 August 1950 with the 4.39pm from Eastbourne. *J. J. Smith, courtesy Bluebell Railway Museum*

Cuckoo Line Memories 2
Richard 'Dick' Brown

Interviewed by David Vaughan

Dick Brown was born in 1944 in the railway cottages at Rotherfield. 'Dad was the signalman at Rotherfield station, so you could say I was born on the railway. The first thing I remember about the railway – and it is a vivid memory – was looking down on the goods yard from my bedroom window and seeing a train being loaded with military vehicles and guns. It was soon after the war had finished and I think it must have been the army removing the stuff from the anti-aircraft battery that had been up in the forest nearby.

'We used to go everywhere by walking the line – everybody on the line knew who we were, the linesmen and the engine crews. In fact, they often used to give us a lift on the engine.

Dick Brown aged 15. *Dick Brown collection*

On Saturdays I used to go down to the goods yard and ride on the engine while they shunted the yard. On Sundays I would go with my Dad to change all the signal lamps [the oil lamps that illuminated the signals had to be cleaned and refilled on a regular basis] because on a Sunday there was a two-hour gap between the trains, which meant we could go as far as the distant signal and work our way back.

DV: 'Didn't your parents worry about you being on the line?'

DB: 'Oh no, we knew where to walk safely and when all the trains were due. In fact, the railway was our playground. We used to make camps in the culverts under the track. I remember getting told off by the p-way man because we lit a camp fire and the smoke came up through the sleepers and gave us away! There was a door into a big room space under the up platform and we used to go in there to play and at weekends we would get under the doors at the good shed and play on the boxes and crates in there and use the shed crane as a swing.'

DV: 'The goods yard sounds like a busy one. What sort of traffic did it handle?'

DB: 'All sorts. There were "Jiffy pots" [a local horticultural product made from fibre for seedlings], mushrooms, coal, cattle, various stuff for local shops and businesses and quite a few horse boxes, which were usually attached to passenger trains. The train used to have to run round, go in the yard, pick up the horse box put it on the back of the train and run round again. If it was a down train, I used to go with my Dad and, using pinch bars, we would move the horse box along until it was clear of the points at the entrance to the yard, then all the driver would have to do was propel back and pick it up. This would save at least 20 minutes of running-round time.

Another thing was that, although Rotherfield had a water crane, there was no sign of a water tank. That was because there were two 48,000-gallon tanks under our garden that were filled naturally from a spring. Before we got a proper mains supply, we used the water for the sink and all our washing. The tanks were gravity fed and we used to go inside them when they were occasionally cleaned out. They were like cathedrals with big brick arches. The garden was higher than the station, so the water crane could also be gravity fed, hence there was no need for an above-ground tank. The drivers used to like our water because it was pure spring water. They were supposed to fill up at Heathfield, but that was hard water, so they preferred to fill up at Rotherfield.

I remember one time when an up train didn't fill up at Heathfield and he hit a landslip in the cutting coming out of Argos Hill Tunnel. They pulled the coaches back and fortunately no one was hurt, but the passengers had to walk back along the line. The engine meanwhile was stuck in the slip and they had to dig the front end out. By the time they got it back to Rotherfield it was very low on water but they couldn't get into the platform to the water crane because the front end steps had got bent out in the collision, so my Dad came running up saying, "Quick, get all the hoses," so we got all the garden hoses from the cottages and hooked them all up and connected them to the tap in the gents toilet. They were just long enough to get to the tank on the engine, so he didn't have to chuck the fire out in the platform. The driver's name was Peter Ayman and he remembered me for that day many years later, when I was involved in an accident at Earlswood.'

DV: 'So you often used to help out even though you were still at school?'

DB: 'Oh yes, we did. When I was 14 I remember that Fred Critall, one of the other Rotherfield signalmen, had a bad back and couldn't pull the levers. Well, there wasn't much in the way of sick pay then, so I and my mate Richard, who lived next door and was the son of the Redgate Mill Junction signalman, used to work the box while Fred was lying flat out with his bad back on the floor behind us. He filled in the train register book of course. Often two trains would cross at the station, which made changing the train staffs easy, but if we had to give the staff to the up train, we would use a bike to ride along the platform to give him the staff. All the drivers knew us and we often had lifts in the guard's van up in the "birdcage".

More than often we would ride in the cab. In fact, when I went to see my aunt, who lived in Muswell Hill, my Mum sent me up on the 9am train from Rotherfield that had two coaches and went right through to Victoria, where my aunt would meet me under the clock. I rode all the way to Upper Warlingham, just before we joined the main line, then I would have to get down off the footplate and ride in the carriage. I would have been no more than eight years old then – you couldn't let a kid do that now.

Going back to the early days at Rotherfield: one thing I remember was the coal merchant who had the coal bins in the yard and whose name was Pollington. Now, if he had a couple of wagons that he had not had time to unload, he would have to pay the railway what they called demurrage. There was a man called Dodds, and Pollington paid him overtime to unload the wagons at night so he didn't have to pay the railway. Well, Dodds used to pay me and my mate Richard half-a-crown to go down to the coal yard and unload instead; in the meantime, Dodds would nip off down the pub! Well, it was all right at first if the bins were empty because we would drop the door of the wagon and a lot of the coal would just fall out, but if they were full up you had to shovel all 14 tons out. This took us all evening and my Mum went mad because we used to go home black all over with coal dust.

On Saturdays I used to go down the yard and go on the footplate of the engine that was shunting. Well, one Saturday I was on this old "C" Class and the fireman, Stan Laycock, went off with some of the other blokes down the pub so I was firing, but just as I was putting a shovel full of coal in the box the driver opened the regulator and the draught sucked the shovel out of my hand and went straight in the firebox. Well, we couldn't get it back so we looked all around for another shovel but couldn't find one, so when Stan came back from the pub to finish his shift he had to go all the way to Tunbridge Wells chucking the coal in by hand. Many years later, Stan had graduated to a driver on electrics and every time he saw me along the line he would shout out, "You were the bugger who lost my shovel!"

Between October and March, Dad and I used to do what was called cut and clear. This was in the days when you used to keep the cuttings and embankments clear – no leaves on the line then. This involved cutting back all the trees, brambles and bushes over an area of 10 chains (220 yards) from Rotherfield towards Heathfield. From that, Dad made up bundles of pea sticks and bean poles and sold them all round the local villages. Of course we never went short of wood for the fire. On a Sunday, when there was a two-hour gap between trains, we would get a trolley and go down the line collecting all the larger wood cuttings and take them back to the yard. When we moved later to Hampden Park, we filled two 16-ton mineral wagons with all our wood and got them sent down to the yard there, where we unloaded them. When we finished work each day we would go to the yard and carry it home a bit at a time. We had enough firewood to last two years.'

DV: 'So you started work officially for the railway in 1960 when you were 15 years old. Where was that?'

DB: 'I started at Tunbridge Wells [signalling] depot as an apprentice. It was a five-year apprenticeship. To start with, I did ten months with the mechanical fitters, which involved various areas of work, then it was six months with the pole gang on the railway's own telegraph and phone lines, then six months each with the mechanical linesman, the electrical linesman, then the crew that did new works, then another six-month stint with the locking fitters [signal box interlocking mechanisms] and six more with the telephone exchange fitters, a job that also involved ticket machines, railway clocks and even the platform lifts, so that way you covered everything. I remember that when I was on the pole gang on the Cuckoo Line we were putting in colour light distant signals between Heathfield and Horam – this would have been in 1962. We were running the lines in for the battery-operated repeater circuits; later on, with the electrical fitters, we put in track circuits, but that was only just before they closed the line and they never got to use them.

One job that came up about every six weeks on the Cuckoo Line was due to the fact that there were more up trains than down trains, particularly on Saturdays, so the train staffs from up trains used to build up in the machines in the signal boxes. Two of us had to start at Redgate Mill and take all the extra staffs out of their machine, get on a train down to Rotherfield and take out their extra staffs, replacing them with the ones from Redgate Mill Junction. The signalman had to sign for them of course. We then took those down to the next box and repeated the operation. We did this all the way down to Polegate. It took us two days because we did it all by train, there were no permanent way road vans in those days.

I remember one time when I was with the pole gang at Heathfield they had just redone the tarmac surface on the platform. A mate and I were working on a pole at the end of the platform using strap-on leg irons. These were similar to those used by GPO linesmen and had spikes fitted that gripped the pole. The user would work up the pole using these with a strap around his waist. Anyway, we were having a race to see who could get up the pole the fastest. I won but on the way back down the strap broke and I went sliding down the pole straight into the wet tarmac and my boot became stuck fast in it!

There was a ganger at Horam called Charlie Brown. When we were doing the bases for the colour light signals, Charlie was making the concrete for them in the goods yard. It was some sort of quick-drying concrete and he was making it up in barrels as needed. He had just made a batch and asked the signalman if it was all right after the next train to use the trolley we were using to go down the line with it. The signalman said OK but what he didn't tell him was that the next train was the goods, so, when it went in to shunt the yard, poor Charlie could not get his trolley with the barrels of cement out and it set hard. He didn't half create about that, I can tell you! As well as the dairy at Horam, there was a market garden that supplied all its flowers for Woolworths stores in the London area, so the 2 o'clock train had vans that were all loaded with fresh flowers.

Another thing about the Cuckoo Line was that all the staff had other jobs: Dad used to work on a farm when he wasn't in the box. At Horam one bloke was a chimney sweep and used to nip off on his bike between trains to do a local chimney. The signalman at Horam used to go and work at the Express Dairy repairing their equipment. The dairy had a rail siding for tankers and sometimes in the winter, when there were not so many trains, he would nip out between them and do a bit in the dairy. Another chap, Jack Pocock, who lived in a cottage at Rotherfield, used to make dolly clothes pegs, whittling away at them in the signal box at Redgate Mill between trains. Later, when I was working with a lineman from Groombridge replacing point rodding, we worked all the way down to Polegate, but when I went to Redgate Mill Junction signal box where Jack worked, I went under the box to do some work and it was full with "pimps" of hazel wood that Fred had stacked up to dry over the winter in readiness to make his clothes pegs.'

DV: 'What was the Cuckoo Line like to work on generally?'

DB: 'It was a nice little line. We never had any road vehicles to get from job to job in those days; instead we had a four-wheel rail van, a "GUV" [General Utility Van No DS 120] that we used to park in Heathfield or Horam yard and then we'd walk to wherever we had to get to. The train drivers always stopped to give us a lift, especially if we were carrying gear. In those days everybody mucked in and helped everybody else out – there was none of this, "Oh you can't do that, it's not your job." We would help clear the platforms of ice in the winter and if we were walking along the platform and saw a door open on the train, we would close it.

If you were working along the line and you wanted coal for the p-way hut stove you would hold up a lump of coal so the train crew would see you and the fireman would chuck down a lump of coal. Well, I remember one time when the lump he chucked down was so big it nearly knocked down the door of the hut! We put it on the fire as it was and it took nearly three days to burn through.

The railway telegraph pole routes were vital means of communication. There were four telephone lines on the Cuckoo Line route plus the repeater lines for the signals and the block instruments between the signal boxes. The network needed a lot of regular maintenance as a break in the line would bring things to a stop, so it was important to get the connection re-established as soon as possible. Now, the repeaters had earth returns and you could get all sorts of problems that were tricky to trace. One of the tricks we had if there was a broken wire was this: the poles all had lightning conductors with copper wire from the metal cap on the pole running down the side of the pole. We would take this off and connect it to the wire lineside fencing. It did not run to earth because the SR had concrete, not wooden, fence posts, which separated the strands of fencing wire. We then went to the other end of the break and did the same, so a temporary connection was made while we fixed the break in the main cable. It might have been temporary but you didn't have to wait three or four hours for a p-way team run by a sub-contractor to come out and fix it like you do today.'

Mayfield

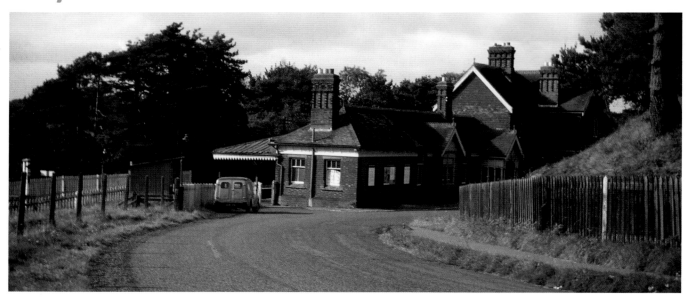

The approach to the station at Mayfield was similar to that at the previous station, Rotherfield. Little changed over the years, save for the type of lamps and fencing, and the position of the various advertising hoardings. As at all the stations, the main buildings also provided accommodation for the resident station master although, with economy already in vogue long before the Second World War, just two Cuckoo Line stations then had a man in residence. The *Southern Railway Magazine* for 1935 afforded the following details: 'Rotherfield – see Eridge', 'Mayfield – see Heathfield', 'Heathfield – Arthur Powell', 'Horam – see Heathfield', 'Hellingly – see Hailsham', 'Hailsham – A. J. Turner'. In each case the supervising man would be expected to pay regular visits to his 'outstations', almost certainly on pay-day. The vacated former station accommodation was invariably made available to another railwayman upon payment of the appropriate rent. *Terry Cole*

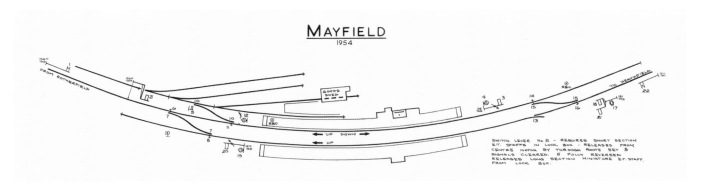

Signal box diagram, Mayfield.

Quiet times at Mayfield. On an unknown date, but possibly in 1931, when the open-air lever frame was provided, the signalling at Mayfield was also rearranged to allow 'long-section' working between Rotherfield and Heathfield. A special miniature staff was provided to cover this working. Signals would then be pulled off in both directions and all trains would use the down platform. A similar arrangement of an open-air lever frame was provided at Sheffield Park on what is now the Bluebell Railway. *Terry Cole*

Opposite bottom: Looking south through the station at Mayfield with the entrance the subway between the platforms visible. A board crossing was also provided at the south end of the platforms for the use of trolleys and barrows. Visible under the canopy is the replacement 'signal box', basically an open-air lever frame that was later given a brick surround and backed on to the booking office. When provided – see the picture overleaf – the single line instruments were moved into the adjacent booking office. The canopy will be seen to be showing signs of settlement over the years. *Terry Cole*

The open-air 22-lever frame at the station as originally provided in 1931. A similar arrangement was made at Horam around the same time. This modification likely allowed for a member of staff to be dispensed with as the role could now be combined as 'porter-signalman' (the term sometimes used is signal/porter, but it means the same thing). *National Railway Museum*

'H' Class 0-4-4T No 31309 enters the station with a northbound train using the down platform: note that No 16 signal on the bracket above the train is in the 'off' position. One of the peculiarities about the stations both here and at Rotherfield was that a refreshment room was provided at both. This also goes some way to explain the length of the buildings at both locations, exemplified in the opening view of this section. When, and for how long, these facilities existed is not reported, although they may possibly have been even from earliest times; here at Mayfield the facilities were certainly in use in 1923. Alan Elliott (the expert on the Cuckoo Line) asks the question why such provision should have been made at these two but not at the other stations. The train is the 5.56pm Eastbourne to Tunbridge Wells West on 8 June 1951. *J. J. Smith, courtesy Bluebell Railway Museum*

Also at the south end we see 'I3' No 32083 (another engine depicted earlier), this time with the 1.50pm Tunbridge Wells West to Eastbourne on 2 June 1951. The '34' post indicates the mileage from Eastbourne. Because of steep gradients on either side of the station, trap points were provided in the up platform line at the south end of the station and these are clearly visible on the left-hand side opposite the second coach of the train. Again, notice the derricks between the sleepers on the single running line; the line on the right forms an over-run. The underbridge immediately at the end of the platform crosses Lewes Road, running at 90° to the railway. *J. J. Smith, courtesy Bluebell Railway Museum*

Hard to imagine now, but there was for many years substantial milk traffic from the station. As an example, in 1928 the station despatched 306,000 gallons, equivalent to 840 gallons each day. At the time, the standard conical churn – introduced because its wider base would make it less likely to fall over in transit – held 17 gallons. An average day would therefore see in the order of 49 full churns dealt with at the station together with the equivalent number of empties being returned. It is likely that this milk was processed a few miles south at the Express Dairies processing plant at Horam. This amount of traffic would have warranted at least one van attached to a passenger working. Seen here with what appears to be a van at the end of the formation, 'I3' No 32022 enters the station from the south in 1949. *S. C. Nash, Stephenson Locomotive Society collection*

DEMU No 1304 pauses at the station forming a Tonbridge to Eastbourne working on a wet 17 April 1965. The porter/signalman is seen passing the staff to the driver for the next section to Heathfield. *Andrew Muckley*

Near Mayfield, another green DEMU set threads its way through the countryside. Notwithstanding the red 'blanks' showing in the route indicator panels, the steam-age oil tail lamp may be noted. *Terry Cole*

Worth mentioning is that c1950 Messrs J. Brockhouse & Co Ltd of Wolverhampton laid down an experimental monorail system north-east of Mayfield station running for about a mile. The construction involved a concrete base approximately 3 feet wide, in the centre of which was a single rail. There is a reference to this in *Industrial Railways and Locomotives of Sussex & Surrey*, compiled by Frank Jux and Roger Hateley and published by the Industrial Railway Society in 2015. From this source we are told that a 2-4-2 diesel power tractive unit (locomotive?) was used fitted with a 90hp Meadows engine. Guide rollers below the axle gripped the centre rails to steer the vehicle, and rubber-tyred wheels were also fitted. The idea was for a 'Uniline Transport System'. Messrs Cambrian Models on their website http://cambrianmodels.co.uk/esxdetls.html have a picture of the locomotive together with the following information:

'The idea was taken up by J. Brockhouse & Co Ltd, and the Executive Engineer of the Company, Mr R. E. Hagley, produced designs for a locomotive, vehicles, and track. The system was called the "Uniline" and a demonstration was given at Mayfield in Sussex, where the experimental track was built, on 6 April 1951. The track, as in the Indian trials, was some 3 feet wide and the stock had a similar guiding system with vertical rollers at front and rear. All vehicles were fitted with pneumatic tyres. In the course of the demonstration on the half-mile track loads of 21 tons were hauled up a gradient of 1 in 15 at a speed of 4½mph.

'Drawings lent to us by J. Brockhouse & Co Ltd show the locomotive used to have been, in railway parlance, a 2-4-2 with a 90bhp four-cylinder diesel engine. It was 15ft 9in over the buffers, which were single and central, and the wheelbase was 10 feet; the leading and trailing wheels had tyres 24in x 7in and the driving wheel tyres were 27in x 7in. There were four guide roller sets arranged in pairs in front of and behind the leading and trailing wheels. The total weight in working order was 5 tons.

'The primary gearbox was a Meadows type 10 four-speed box with clutch and provision for power take-off. It was not fitted with a reverse gear. The secondary gearbox was a "Brockhouse" single-speed and reverse gearbox provided with a jackshaft and coupling rod final drive. The two gearboxes were connected by a flexible coupling. All tyres were inflated at a pressure of 90psi. The locomotive was designed to take curves of 50-foot radius. Compensated brakes were fitted to each axle and an air compressor, reservoir, and driver's brake valve were provided to allow continuous automatic brakes to be used on the train vehicles.

'The drawings show 3-ton vehicles with four wheels, 4½-ton vehicles with six, 6-ton vehicles with eight, and 10-ton vehicles with two six-wheel bogies. The calculated performance figures with the locomotive mentioned showed that up to 25mph might be attained with a suitable load, and in first gear a load of 126 tons might be hauled on the level. Mr Hagley said at the demonstration that the system had not been designed to compete with existing road or rail transport systems, but to supplement them…'

The information is quoted as having been supplied by Paul Kidger. There is also a fascinating film of the experiment in action at http://www.britishpathe.com/video/road-rail-line.

Despite this raft of information, one question does still remain, which is a how and why this Wolverhampton-based engineering company came to be involved in the system, and likewise why it should be trialled in Sussex. *S. C. Nash, Stephenson Locomotive Society collection*

Although intended for freight duties, 'Q1' No 33031 has a turn working a passenger service on the line in 1950. *S. C. Nash, Stephenson Locomotive Society collection*

Another view taken near Mayfield shows 'J2' No 32326 (previously seen at Rotherfield) on a light three-coach train in 1950. At some time in the recent past concrete sleepers have been offloaded ready for relaying. *S. C. Nash, Stephenson Locomotive Society collection*

South of Mayfield, 'E5' 0-6-2T No 32405 works the 5.55pm Tunbridge Wells West to Eastbourne service on 23 August 1951. Three months later this engine was withdrawn from service, one of ten of the class to go that year, which left fifteen in service, the last four being withdrawn in January 1956. *J. J. Smith, courtesy Bluebell Railway Museum*

South of Mayfield towards Heathfield the railway continued on its way of sharp curves and steep gradients, and it was between these two stations that an accident occurred on 1 September 1897, which at the enquiry was put down to poor track. The engine in question was LBSCR 'D1' Class 0-4-2T No 297 *Bonchurch*, which was in charge of the 8.18am Eastbourne to Tunbridge Wells service. The train had been heading north and had reached the bottom of Tooth's Bank when '...the engine suddenly rolled violently and flung itself and the carriages off the track with a thunderous crash audible for a distance of 1½ miles.' *Noodle Books collection*

Considering where the engine landed, it is not surprising that the driver, James McKenly, died before help could arrive. Fireman Lewis Minns was severely injured, although he was able to extricate himself from the wreck. *Noodle Books collection*

The train consisted of six vehicles, all four- and six-wheeled stock. All six vehicles left the rails and 30 passengers out of an unknown total were injured. Several of those travelling were also railwaymen and later stated that they knew the line to be 'rough' at this point, particularly when travelling north. The locomotive on recovery duty is LBSCR 'D3' 0-4-4T No 381 *Fittleworth*. *Noodle Books collection*

At the subsequent enquiry, attention quickly shifted away from any potential defect with the locomotive or rolling stock to the track. This was in poor shape with rotting sleepers and irregular elevation on the curves. It was also pointed out that the train was running 4 minutes late on its schedule and the driver may well have been attempting to make up some time to maintain a connection at Groombridge, where the last two vehicles were due to be detached and continue on as a connection to London. Speedometers were not fitted to engines then (some would never have one fitted), although in the opinion of the railway staff the train had derailed when travelling at a speed around 40mph. The conclusion was that the speed of the train allied to the state of the track and curvature were all contributory. Apart from a recommendation that track maintenance be improved (much of the line was hurriedly relaid), additional time was allowed for trains between stations, not just between Mayfield and Heathfield, while warning boards were also erected on either side of the derailment. Any attempt by crews to make up time was also to be prohibited. *Noodle Books collection*

Heathfield

Approaching Heathfield from the north, 'Q' Class 0-6-0 No 30534 is on a passenger service in 1949. The signal is the Heathfield down distant, by this stage fixed at caution but at one time a working arm.
S. C. Nash, Stephenson Locomotive Society collection

Near the same spot is another member of the 'I3' Class, No 32077, in 1950. Twenty-seven members of this class were built at Brighton between 1907 and 1913. The first to go was in 1944, after which withdrawals began in earnest in 1950 with no fewer than seventeen taken out of service in 1951. No 32077 was one that went in that year, to leave just a single survivor, No 32091, ironically the last built. *S. C. Nash, Stephenson Locomotive Society collection*

This time it is SR Class 'I1X' No 2002, yet to receive its '3' prefix and previously seen at Tunbridge Wells West on page 14. The engine is leaving the north end of Heathfield Tunnel bound for Mayfield in 1951. *S. C. Nash, Stephenson Locomotive Society collection*

Also emerging from the northern end of Heathfield Tunnel is 'H' Class 0-4-4T No 31279, bearing a St Leonards (74E) shed code. On this occasion the working is not reported, although the photographer did record the time as 4.39pm on 4 June 1951. It will be noted that although there is provision for a second line of rails, only a single track passes through the tunnel. Note the signal wires: these led to signals 10 and 21 respectively, affording 'wrong road' working into the up platform and, more usually, the down home signal. *J. J. Smith, courtesy Bluebell Railway Museum*

From the south end of the 265-yard tunnel (slight variations in length occur in various publications, likely due to which side of the 34-chain curve the measurement was taken) we get a view of the gas plant – which will be described later – and the station on 10 June 1965. Apart from a very short siding primarily intended to serve the former facility, goods yard facilities here were at the south end of the station site. *J. J. Smith, courtesy Bluebell Railway Museum*

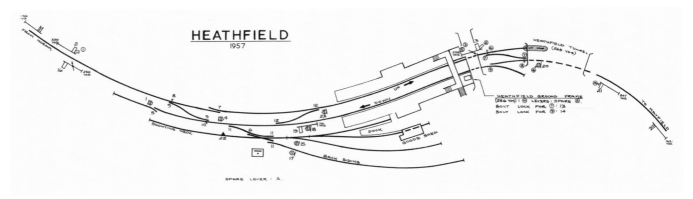

Signal box diagram, Heathfield.

In 1920 an accident occurred at Heathfield, when a passenger train was derailed as it left the station on its way south. The incident occurred as a result of previous damage to the points concerned. Fortunately a full report from the Ministry of Transport survives and, apart from providing information about the actual occurrence, affords a fascinating glimpse of what was at the time a very busy railway. The reader may find it convenient to refer to the signal box diagram when following the accompanying text. However, please note that, while the track layout is the same, the diagram was made after the Inspector's recommendations were implemented. Signal 1 and trap 5 were *not* present in 1920. With the exception of reference 'A', the other signal referred to and point numbers still apply.

'Sir,
I have the honour to report for the information of the Minister of Transport, in accordance with the order of the 4th May, the result of my enquiry into the circumstances of a derailment which occurred at about 7.32pm, on the 19th April, at Heathfield, on the London, Brighton and South Coast Railway.

In this case, the 6.45pm down passenger train from Tunbridge Wells to Eastbourne, after having stopped at Heathfield, was proceeding from the down loop to the single line, when the engine and the two leading coaches were derailed, all wheels, at the facing points of the over-run siding.

Two passengers complained of shock. Both tongue rails of the points were damaged, and a number of fish bolts and chairs were broken. The train consisted of three bogie composite coaches with a six-wheeled brake at each end. It was drawn by Tank Engine No 616, 0-4-2 type, total weight in working order 43 tons 10 cwt. The engine and train were fitted with Westinghouse brake, operating brake blocks on all wheels with the exception of the centre pairs on the six-wheeled vehicles.

Description
Heathfield is situated on the Company's single-line branch about midway between Tunbridge Wells at the northern end and Eastbourne at the southern end. The general direction of the station platforms is north-south, the down loop being to the east of the up loop. From the southern end of the station the line towards Eastbourne is on a curve of about 1,500 feet radius to the west.

The goods yard, situated to the east of the line, takes off the down loop by means of a trailing connection some 370 feet south of the platforms. The south signal box (containing 23 working levers), situated east of the down loop, controls the connections and the signals at this end of the station.

An over-run siding, about 500 feet clear, is provided at this end of the station in extension of the down loop. It was at the over-run facing points (No 9) that the derailment occurred. The line through the station, up to about these points, is on a falling gradient towards Eastbourne of 1 in 304. From here southwards the grade increases to 1 in 50 round the curve. The whole of the over-run siding except a short length at its southern end is on the grade.

The relative points, signals, etc, concerned and their approximate distance from the centre of the South signal box are as follows:

North end of platforms	750 feet North
South end of platforms	270 feet North
Down starting signal No 19	235 feet North

Trailing crossover No 12 between up and down loop lines:

Points in up line and disc No 23	245 feet North
Points in down line and disc No 4	35 feet North

Trailing points No 11 and disc A in down loop leading to goods yard

	110 feet South

Facing crossover No 9, between down loop and main line:

Over-run points in down loop	160 feet South
Loop points in main line	380 feet South
Dead end of over-run siding	850 feet South

The points (No 9) on which the derailment occurred are equipped, in accordance with the Company's standard practice, with the Saxby-Farmer locking bar connections and the Kirby detector situated between the tongue rails. The weight of rail is 96lbs per yard. The tongues are formed out of 30 feet rails and are connected together with five stretcher rods. In addition a sixth split-blade is provided for bolting and detecting the tongue.

Conclusion

1. This is an exceptional case of the failure of approved detecting apparatus to indicate the points were not in a fit state for the passage of a train in the facing direction after they had been run through by a previous train in the trailing direction. This does not mean that the detection mechanism is open to criticism. It was in fact due to its strength that the apparatus permitted the starting signal to be lowered, and therefore failed to indicate to either the signalman or driver that anything was amiss.

The train in question, having received the single line staff, had started from the down platform with starting and advanced starting signals cleared and had attained a speed, it was stated, of some 3 or 4 miles per hour, when, on reaching facing points No 9 leading from the down loop to the over-run dead-end siding, the engine straddled the tongue rails and became derailed, causing the two leading coaches to leave the road.

2. The following is briefly an account of the movement prior to the accident:

The 5.55pm down passenger train from Tunbridge Wells arrived on the down loop at Heathfield at 6.49pm. The engine was uncoupled and ran round the train. On receipt of a flag signal from Porter Signalman Leeves, who was on duty in the south box at the time, the train was then propelled over points No 9, in their normal position, into the over-run siding, to wait there to make the 7.48pm return train to Tunbridge Wells.

Leeves then had to deal with the 6.25pm up passenger train, which arrived on the up loop from Eastbourne at 7.09pm. This train is booked to return to Eastbourne and had two horse boxes in rear for Heathfield. The engine was therefore detached and ran round to the rear of the train. The two horse boxes were shunted via No 11 points into the loading dock in the back of the bay platform, and the engine returned to the rear of the train. Leeves then set the road by pulling points 9 and the bar 10, which locks them, for the shunt movement, for which he cleared disc signal 23, for the train to proceed from the up loop to the down loop and on to the main line via the facing crossover No 9. The train was then propelled into the goods yard to await its return journey to Eastbourne. This movement was completed about 7.23pm.

In the meanwhile Leeves had accepted, at 7.13pm, the 6.45pm train from Tunbridge Wells – that concerned in the accident – and it had already left Mayfield, the next station, when, in order to comply with the regulations, he proceeded at about 7.23pm, when the last movement was completed, to clear the over-run siding before allowing the 6.45pm train to approach the station. He accordingly pulled disc signal No 4 and gave Wheatley, the driver of the train standing in this siding (the 5.55 pm) a hand signal to leave the siding for the up loop. Wheatley, running tender first, brought the train out,

traversing points No 9 in the trailing direction and the crossover 12 in the facing direction, and ran to the water column on the up line.

Leeves then put back disc No 4, replaced crossover No 12 to normal, and cleared the signals for the 6.45pm train, which arrived about 7.30pm and left at 7.32pm. Driver Gutsell of this train stated that he was not held up at the home signals and that he found the starting signal clear when he arrived at the platform.

Leeves stated that it was not until he came on duty the next day that he "began to realise that this train was derailed through No 9 points having been run through trailing by a previous movement."

3. On examination after the accident it was found that the only damage affecting the points, from which conclusions can be drawn as to the cause of the derailment, occurred to the tongue rails. The outside tongue, viz, the one lying against the stock rail as the 5.55pm train drew out of the over-run siding, was broken away at the head to a depth of some 1½ inches for a length of about 12 inches near the tip. The tip itself for a distance of 2 inches was not damaged. The tongue rail was bent about 1½ inches towards the centre of the track at the point of damage, but the tip remained in its proper position against the stock rail, and the detector rod was not bent or displaced. The other tongue was broken away at the top at a distance of 1 foot 5 inches from the tip for a length of 5 inches and to a depth of 2½ inches. This tongue was bent to the same extent outwards, from the centre of the track at the point of damage, and its detector rod was also undamaged.

The points were locked (lever No 10) at the time of the movement from the over-run siding was made. Driver Wheatley stated in his evidence that, owing to the heavy rising gradient of 1 in 50, he could not have passed over the points at more than 3 miles per hour. He was running tender first and, with the engine working hard, he neither heard nor felt anything unusual.

It is obvious, I think, that the engine gently pushed its way through the points, the thin portions of which, at the tips, broke away as described. These points are of particularly rigid construction and the blow at this low speed was not sufficient to cause the detector rodding or stretchers to buckle, nor to damage in any way the casting of the Kirby detector through which the rods pass. It was due to this that the detector slide mechanism did not obstruct the movement of the starting signal wire, and that, therefore, immediately after the movement, Leeves was able to pull the signal.

The tips of the tongues were properly set but the flange of the near-side leading wheel of the engine must have encountered the false nose due to the inward bend of the tongue on that side. The flange was assisted in crossing the tongue rail at this point by the gap (1½ inches in depth) in the head which had broken away. The engine took the general direction of the over-run siding, the inner rail of which acted as a guide.

4. From the forgoing it will be seen that, from 6.49pm, the time the first train arrived, till 7.30pm, there was considerable, though not unusual, movement in this single line station. I am satisfied that Signalman Leeves had no knowledge at the time that the points in question were not fit for traffic. Inadvertently he must have made the initial mistake of failing to set these points in the proper position for the engine and coaches of the 5.55pm train to leave the over-run siding. It appears that when he came to lower the signals for the 6.45pm train, he was not reminded by the reverse position of the levers 9 and 10 of this initial mistake or, therefore, of the possibility of the points having thereby been damaged. The fact that he was able to lower his starting signal proves that he was not warned by the detection apparatus that anything was wrong with the points. His evidence was given in a straightforward manner, and though responsible for the damage done to the points, I consider that, in the special circumstances of the failure of the detecting apparatus to give him notice of this damage, he is absolved from further blame. He has 20 years service with the Company and has been at Heathfield for 8 years.

Neither of the engine drivers can be held responsible – Wheatley for the damage to the points, or Gutsell for the subsequent derailment.

5. The accident would probably not have happened had the movement from the over-run siding been controlled by a trap and a disc signal (led by either of the existing discs Nos 4 or A dependent upon the setting of the road), instead of a by-hand signal from the cabin. On this turns the question of the use to which the over-run siding is being put. Traffic at this station is heavy and the siding has to be used for marshalling the goods train daily. Leeves states that he kept the siding as clear as possible, but he was at times obliged to continue shunting thereon and accept a down train at the same time. He occasionally had to stand stock with an engine at the far end on this siding, but it is not customary to use the siding for stabling stock.

I recommend that this siding be recognised in future as a shunting neck for the goods yard, and that it be equipped with trap points and a disc as described above. This will reduce the present clear over-run length, 1,085 feet from the starting signal to, say, 585 feet. In view of the fact that all trains stop here, and that there has been no trouble in the past, I consider that, having regard to economy, this reduced length will be sufficient for safety. I understand from the Company's representatives, with whom I discussed various alternatives, that they propose to carry out this work, which will involve extra levers in the cabin.

A Mount. Major RE'

'C2X' No 32551, fitted with a single-dome boiler, emerges from Heathfield Tunnel with a freight from Tunbridge Wells West on 17 May 1950. All the available evidence points to the fact that the left-hand line was only ever a headshunt, at one time extending some distance into the tunnel but in later years cut back as seen here. To some extent this is contradicted by a reference made by J. T. Howard-Turner in his trilogy on the history of the LBSCR, which implies that the headshunt may have been extended through the tunnel during the Second World War in the form of an extended loop. This cannot be confirmed and, on the available photographic evidence, would appear unlikely. *J. J. Smith, courtesy Bluebell Railway Museum*

Heathfield station looking north c1890. Originally intended to be named 'Cross in Hand', the 17½ miles of new railway from Hailsham had arrived here on 5 April 1880. Eventually both names would appear on the running-in boards, although in the final years a simplified 'Heathfield' was again used. The station was approximately midway between Tunbridge Wells and Eastbourne and was also considered to be the most important of the stopping places. That said, passenger trains on the Cuckoo Line always called at all stations. As built, the railway was some distance from the town but, unlike elsewhere, this did not prove an obstacle as the town would expand over the years to meet the railway. At the north end of the platforms and just prior to the tunnel, an overbridge carried what is nowadays designated the A265 Lewes to Hawkhurst road over the railway. It was on this roadway that the main station buildings, again in the style of Myres, were provided. Passengers would use the road overbridge to cross between the platforms protected by a covered way when making their way to and from the down side, but with no such cover available for access to the up platform.

Although this image is purported to be dated c1890, we may wonder if it is not some time earlier judging by the incomplete state of the platform surface, which would surely have drawn criticism from the Board of Trade Inspector, who would have had to sanction the line as fit for traffic prior to passengers being carried. The yard would appear well-stocked with goods vehicles, still not unusual if this is in fact prior to opening, for it was practice to work freight trains only at first, the passage of which would assist in the consolidation of the earthworks. Finally, note the ballast covering of the sleepers, common practice at the time and believed to have advantage in preventing movement as well as allowing a horse to walk more easily. This was later discontinued when it became apparent that timber rot could set in and not be immediately obvious. *Madgwick Collection*

Below: This second early image of the station is slightly later, with a small tank engine, No 298 (another member of the 'D1' Class), arriving with a southbound train. Whether this was a special working of sorts is open to discussion as there appear to be several members of staff stood almost sentinel-like against the canopy supports – note also the signalman with the 'staff' under his arm (the railwayman nearest the camera). There also appears to be a distinct lack of public present. The coaching stock is either to Stroudley or Craven design, the majority likely to be of the four-wheel type but typical of what was used on the line and indeed on numerous other LBSCR branch/cross-country routes at this time. Finally, note how the sleepers are now mainly exposed, with their covering of ballast removed. *Madgwick Collection*

Above: At road level we have a view of the main building, albeit in BR days. The bookstall was a feather in the station's cap, while years before the resident station master had the common dual role of station master/sub-postmaster.
Hugh Davies, 'Photos from the Fifties'

Left and opposite: At the time of building the railway a borehole was sunk in an attempt to find a water supply both for the station and also for locomotive purposes. In the event this had to be sunk to a depth of 370 feet before an adequate and reliable supply was located. On a different occasion and at a lesser depth, a 'foul smell' had been detected from the drilling, accompanied by a 'hissing' noise. Investigation by means of a lighted candle produced the not-unexpected result of a sheet of flame. A similar result occurred with two separate drillings. Subsequently this gas supply was tapped and used to supply the station and also for pumping purposes, although it had been hoped that such a natural reservoir might be enough to be considered a commercial proposition both locally and elsewhere. This would not be the case, although gas continued to be extracted well into BR days, but mainly taken away for research. The siding seen running into the gas plant was just 25 feet in length and able to accommodate a single wagon.
Noodle Books/J. J. Smith, courtesy Bluebell Railway Museum

Having emerged from the tunnel, No 32551 waits in the down platform with mixed vehicles. As at Mayfield, the canopy is displaying signs of droop. In the background it is possible to discern the former North signal box, retained in use as a ground frame to control the points at the tunnel end of the station. *J. J. Smith, courtesy Bluebell Railway Museum*

Standard Class 4 tank No 80142 emerges from the tunnel and is about to enter the station. The short siding to the gas plant has already been mentioned, but what has not is that this did not posses a catch point of any type so was more likely used as a trap rather than having a vehicle left upon it at any time. *Hugh Davies, 'Photos from the Fifties'*

Devoid of trains on 10 June 1965, we have a clear view of the overbridge – by now devoid of its covering to protect passengers, and the former North signal box, still in use but reclassified as a ground frame. Note the rail-built SR upper-quadrant up starting signal, the curved arm of the water crane – compared with that at Rotherfield – and also the 'S' (Stop) board for all up passenger trains. *J. J. Smith, courtesy Bluebell Railway Museum*

A special working at Heathfield on 17 May 1950. We are not told if the inspection saloon seen was attached to an ordinary train or if this was a special working in its own right. It was not totally uncommon for the divisional engineer/manager to arrange such a working when he might inspect particular locations. ARP painting is also still evident here. *J. J. Smith, courtesy Bluebell Railway Museum*

Alongside a simple running-in nameboard, DEMU No 1309 arrives at Heathfield forming a Tunbridge Wells to Eastbourne service in June 1963. *Real Photographs*

With a pull-push coach set but a non-pull-push-fitted loco, a southbound train headed by a clean Standard Class 4MT leaves the station. The large building to the left and in front of the train is Messrs Strickland's corn mill. *Hugh Davies, 'Photos from the Fifties'*

Looking back through the station the well-stocked goods yard can be seen, consisting of five sidings, including a dock. There was also a goods warehouse – perhaps more commonly referred to as a goods shed – and yard crane. These facilities included a private siding shared by Messrs Strickland and the Heathfield District Poulterers Association – in later years poultry traffic was despatched by passenger train – and local instructions specified that this siding was not to be used for general traffic. Until BR days an average of two wagons daily were received and despatched from the yard. The service train in the background is bound for Eastbourne with a BR Standard Class 4MT at the head of a numbered set of Mk 1 coaches. *Hugh Davies, 'Photos from the Fifties'*

'Working Instructions, Heathfield: Strickland's Siding – This siding leads from the goods yard and holds five wagons. A scotch block, worked from the signal box, is placed at the five-wagon limit and wagons must be kept inside this scotch, which must be in the normal position across the siding before any movement is made from the goods yard to the over-run or single line. This siding is served by ordinary goods services.'

With the roof of the 'South' signal box just visible above the coaches, 'E4' 0-6-2T No 32517 arrives at Heathfield against the late afternoon sun on 16 September 1952. The train is the 4.39pm from Eastbourne to Tunbridge Wells West. *J. J. Smith, courtesy Bluebell Railway Museum*

In standard SR/BR(S) livery, the station is seen looking north c1965. The absence of passengers was an unfortunate precursor to closure. *Terry Cole*

It appears that just a single passenger has alighted from this northbound train, which is just about to leave behind grimy Class 4MT No 80140. *Terry Cole*

Two coaches are also sufficient for this southbound working behind No 80152, recorded around the same time. There was an oft-quoted and unfortunately true phrase from this period that a lack of passengers led to good timekeeping. The '537' on the carriage end refers to what had once been a BR Mk 1 coach set, but seen here in only part formation. *Terry Cole*

The same train is seen again from a wider perspective. Most services on the Cuckoo Line operated throughout the length of the route, but there were in addition some 'short workings' running from Eastbourne to Hailsham and/or Heathfield. As an example, there were two down workings starting from Heathfield in 1965, although due to timetabling both were later involved in a wait of several minutes at Horam while an up train cleared the single line. *Terry Cole*

Diesel power and a yard full of coal – and not much else. This is a scene typical of the railway in its final years. Heathfield would continue to handle coal and any other goods from closure to passengers until 26 April 1968, when a road crane damaged a bridge near Horam and repairs were not considered justified. *Terry Cole*

Diesel power: what would later become known as a 'Class 33' but seen here in the form of No D6501 enters Heathfield from the south with a rake of primarily Maunsell 'Restriction 1' vehicles, although the final carriage appears to be of the wider 'Restriction 4' type. Coaches were associated with various routes, so care had to be taken when marshalling trains. Only 'Restriction 1' vehicles were permitted to operate through the tunnel between Tunbridge Wells West and Tonbridge. This class of diesel locomotive was in charge of most of the final freight services to Heathfield, following closure to passengers. *Real Photographs*

Deep in the Sussex countryside an unidentified three-car 'Sussex' DEMU set is seen near Heathfield. *Roger Holmes*

Super-power in the form of rebuilt Bulleid 'West Country' No 34100 *Appledore* nears Heathfield with the 9.52am from Victoria on 1 October 1961. At times the Cuckoo Line was used both as a diversionary route as well as for sight-seeing trains, both following a practice that went back to the days of the Southern Railway. *J. J. Smith, courtesy Bluebell Railway Museum*

On a special working on 4 August 1963, unrebuilt 'Battle of Britain' No 34057 *Biggin Hill* is in charge of the 11.12am ecs (empty coaching stock) from Heathfield to Polegate. Other than being south of Heathfield, the exact location is not confirmed. Of course the question arises, if the train is returning south, what was the working that had taken it north? *J. J. Smith, courtesy Bluebell Railway Museum*

Just two wagons form the load for 'C2X' No 32538 as it ambles along with a pick-up goods south of Heathfield on 21 April 1951.
J. J. Smith, courtesy Bluebell Railway Museum

LONDON CENTRAL DIVISION

THROUGH THE STATION ALPHABET.— HEATHFIELD.

Heathfield Station was opened on April 5th, 1880, when the branch line was extended there from Hailsham, the extension Heathfield to Eridge being opened on September 1st, 1880, joining up with the Uckfield to Groombridge line, which was opened in 1868. Heathfield's opening coincided with that of Ryde Esplanade, the Ryde Pier extension following in July, 1880. (This by way of digression).

Owing to difficulties of various descriptions encountered in constructing the line, the station was built in Waldron parish, with the signal box in Heathfield, and the station residence and booking office are on a higher level than the platforms, which are reached by a covered corridor, footbridge and stairs.

The original village, with its ancient parish church, is nearly two miles away and consequently the railway development led to the formation of a new business centre, which has been continually enlarged since 1900, so that quite a town lies around the station, constituting the greatest part of the business life of the two parishes, whose present day population approximates 6,000.

The station is situated near the summit of one of the many beautifully wooded ridges of this part of the Weald of Sussex, 15 miles from Eastbourne and a similar distance from Tunbridge Wells. Being well over 500ft. above sea level, one

The entrance to Heathfield tunnel.

Page 12

has only to progress a short way from the station to get splendid views of the surrounding country, extending over the whole of the intervening valley to the South Downs, taking in Pevensey Bay to the east, and the vicinity of Clayton to the west. Northwards are magnificent views of Crowborough, Mayfield and Ashdown Forest, and the wooded country as far as Wadhurst.

HEATHFIELD'S NATURAL GAS.

The line, a single one, takes a falling gradient in each direction for some two miles, being as steep as 1 in 50 in several places, and northwards to Mayfield traverses thickly wooded estates, in which pines predominate. Immediately north of the station a brick tunnel 266 yards long pierces the top of the ridge and contains abundant evidence of the presence of iron in the district, the water which penetrates here being highly coloured with the characteristic colour. Nearby is the 370ft. borehole providing water for station use, and also the natural gas which until recently constituted the lighting agent for the station. Heathfield is unique as the one place in England where a supply of gas, as pure as required for commercial purposes, rises from the earth ready to be stored and utilised. The gas, now termed "Methane", was first discovered in 1896 whilst the borehole was being deepened, and it has been utilised for station lighting until quite recently, when an alternative supply from the local Gas Company was brought into use.

At various times the whole of the natural gas is needed by the Ministry of Mines (Safety in Mines) Research Board, who have had a monopoly of the supply for several years for experimental purposes. A large number of cylinders are regularly filled under compression and forwarded to Harper Hill, Brixton. The gas is odourless, so cannot be used for domestic purposes, although it is remarkably clean in burning. Some of it is also supplied by the Mines Department to Imperial Chemical Industries, Ltd. Its origin is speculative, but it is generally believed to be a product of coal or oil.

INDUSTRIES—ANCIENT AND MODERN.

When the iron industry flourished in Sussex some two centuries ago, Heathfield was one of the busiest centres in cannon manufacture and other branches of a trade long dead as far as the South is concerned. It is at the present time the centre of the poultry fattening industry, which produces the birds sold under the trade name of "Surrey" fowls, and which has flourished in the district for upwards of 80 years. Some 270 tons per annum are sent to London market at an "all-in" rate, covering collection and returned empties, at 1d. per bird. Much similar traffic also passes to Eastbourne, Brighton and other seaside resorts.

About 40,000 passengers use the station annually, exclusive of season ticket holders, whilst some 26,000 parcels are dealt with. The Goods Department handles about 25,000 tons and 5,000 wagons per year, much of the traffic consisting of poultry feeding stuffs. Messrs. Stricklands, and the Heathfield and District Poultry Keepers' Association, Ltd., have large granaries served by private siding. Pedigree poultry, eggs for hatching, and day-old chicks, the latter in thousands, at times form a large proportion of

Southern Railway Magazine

Southern Railway Magazine

The approach to Heathfield Station. The source of the natural gas supply is close to the small flight of steps on the left.

the forwarded passenger train traffic to all parts of Great Britain.

An excellent 9-hole golf course is about three-quarters of a mile from the station, and the cricket and football clubs provide all-the-year-round sport in other directions.

The Cuckmere and the Rother rivers have their sources in the district. A landmark not far from the station is the 70ft. high Gibraltar Tower in Heathfield Park, erected in 1792 to commemorate an achievement of a former owner of the Park, General Elliott, afterwards Lord Heathfield. The Park is not open to the public. Cade Street (two miles) takes its names from the roadside monument there recording the capture of the rebel Jack Cade, in 1450. Heathfield Fair, the traditional releasing time of the cuckoo from the "Old Lady's Basket", there received its grant in the 14th century, hence the local terms "Cuckoo" or "Heffle" Fair and the "Cuckoo Line." The Fair is held on April 14th, but is nothing like the size it used to be.

* * *

WEDDING PRESENTATION.

With the good wishes of her colleagues for her future happiness, Miss Evelyn Gilbert, of the L.C.D.S.O., was recently presented with an oak bureau in view of her marriage on December 22nd. She resigned on December 15th, having been with the Company since March, 1929.

* * *

PARTING HONOUR TO RETIRING LOCO. FOREMAN.—There was a large gathering at the Station Hotel, Horsham, on November 22nd, when a con-

January, 1935.

cert was held in honour of Mr. H. Pollott, Loco. Foreman, who recently retired.

The chair was taken by Driver C. Baker, who was supported by Messrs. E. S. Moore, A. B. MacLeod, H. Buck, J. Richardson, J. P. Maitland, and H Layton. Mr. W. Howie (Mr. Pollott's successor) and P.W. Inspector Caton were also present.

Mr. Moore presented Mr. Pollott, on behalf of the Horsham staff, with an arm-chair, and wished him many years of happy retirement. He spoke highly of Mr. Pollott's good qualities, and his remarks were endorsed by Driver Baker, Mr. Howie, and many others.

Mr. Pollott was much affected when he rose to reply. He thanked them all very much for the gift and their kind words, and he hoped that the same support would be accorded his successor as had been given him.

The concert was much enjoyed by all. Those contributing to the evening's entertainment included Messrs. G. Giles, H. Tullett, R. Redford, H. Rowland, H. Power, G. Groombridge, W. Jupp, and H. Strong. The committee responsible for the arrangements were Messrs. C. Baker, F. Trott, R. Menzies, F. Little and A. Francis.

"ROXANA".

Mr. Pollott.

Page 13

Reported as the 9.05am 'Special Freight' north from Polegate, the train is seen here near Horam behind Brighton-based unrebuilt 'Battle of Britain' No 34055 *Fighter Pilot* on 2 July 1960.
J. J. Smith, courtesy Bluebell Railway Museum

Horam

The delightful rural façade of Horam station. Various name changes over the years had seen it referred to as Horeham Road for Waldron; Horeham Road & Waldron; Waldron & Horeham; and finally, in 1953 under British Railways, simply Horam. Again the main building is similar in style but with the single-storey extension clearly shorter than at Mayfield and Rotherfield because there was no provision for refreshments. As with most (if not all) of the Myres-designed stations of this type, the first floor has been tile-hung in place of the original plaster panelling. This was undertaken very early on due to the ingress of damp. *Terry Cole*

There was no footbridge provided at the station, so passengers were required to cross the line by means of the road bridge, which originally had an open-air wooden staircase on either side, although that on the down side was later replaced by a simple path. Seen late on in the life of the railway, on 12 June 1965, there are several passengers as well as what appear to be two railwaymen opposite each other at the edges of the platforms. There are several details to note: the use of standard SR concrete items – running-in board (with space for the earlier more convoluted names) and lamp posts – the sign for Corrall's coal merchant on the extreme right, the grass bank on the right where once the station name had been displayed in stones in what was the station garden, the obvious evidence of ash and cinders in the 'four-foot', and sadly the general air of decay and pending dereliction. Note also the recent brick-built surround to the platform lever frame. *J. J. Smith, courtesy Bluebell Railway Museum*

Diesel and steam crossing at Horam: the diesel is a down working towards Polegate and the steam train, hauled by Standard Class 4MT No 80141, is on an up working to Tunbridge Wells West. To the right of the approaching steam train was the goods yard, although by this time it found little use other than for coal traffic. As elsewhere, trains arriving from both north and south would have a straight run into the station and a curved exit. The 18-lever platform frame had replaced the former North and South signal boxes in August 1935. It may also have been around this time that the distant signals were fixed at caution; 17 of the 18 levers in the new installation were in use, with just one lever (No 13) designated as 'spare'. The photo was taken on 12 June 1965, the last day of service, with No 80141 bearing an appropriate chalked inscription, 'Farewell to Steam – The Cuckoo Flyer', around the smokebox. With the closure of Tunbridge Wells West steam shed taking place on the same day as services ceased on the Cuckoo Line, several of the Standard Class 4MT locos acquired unofficial names, with certain drivers bestowing on them an honorary knighthood or even an elevation to the peerage. *J. J. Smith, courtesy Bluebell Railway Museum*

Standard Class 4MT No 80142 arrives with a down working at what appears to be a deserted scene. Notwithstanding the engine having worked through from Tunbridge Wells West, the available coal in the bunker appears not to have diminished much, while there is also steam to spare. On the right-hand side, note the rear of the 'S' (Stop) board provided for diesel trains. Although not confirmed, it would also appear that the track in the loading dock at least has been lifted. The view was recorded on 4 June 1965, with just one week of services remaining. *Hugh Davies, 'Photos from the Fifties'*

On 18 August 1957 disgustingly filthy 'Battle of Britain' Class 4-6-2 No 34073 *249 Squadron* is slowing on the approach to the platform with the fireman ready to exchange the single-line staff. The train is a through working, the inter-regional 7.09pm Eastbourne to Romford, comprising former LNER stock. Note the electric lights in use in addition to the standard route discs. *J. J. Smith, courtesy Bluebell Railway Museum*

A light engine working heading south at Horam: No 34055 *Fighter Pilot* (seen earlier on the 9.05am 'Special Freight' working) is now returning to Eastbourne on 2 July 1960. In the foreground is the dairy siding provided for the Express Dairy Company in the 1930s, which generated much traffic. Local milk delivered to the station was also processed at the plant. Railborne milk traffic, in both rail tanks and road vehicles loaded on to rail wagons, was unfortunately lost in the 1950s. *J. J. Smith, courtesy Bluebell Railway Museum*

Sussex 'DEMU' No 1310 (its styling and accommodation differing slightly from the original 'Hampshire' sets) waits at the platform bound for Hailsham and Polegate. The up starting signal seen against the background of the overbridge was perhaps slightly unusual in not having a white background to improve sighting. The station itself was located on a short section of 1 in 264 towards Polegate, after a long descent of 1 in 50 and 1 in 80. This difference in the gradient was, however, short-lived, as the fall continued at 1 in 68/300/66 after the station and on towards Hellingly. *Terry Cole*

Entering the south end of the station, 'H' Class 0-4-4T No 31310 has charge of a three-coach 'birdcage' set forming the 5.56pm Eastbourne to Tunbridge Wells West working on 23 April 1951. Note the three sidings into the goods yard on the right. As will be seen from the signalling diagram, access to these sidings was in the form of a 'kick-back', so shunt moves were usually performed by trains in the down direction
 J. J. Smith, courtesy Bluebell Railway Museum

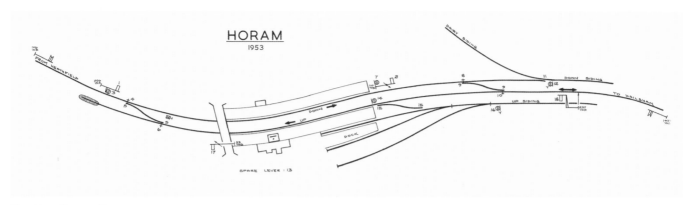

Signal box diagram, Horam.

With the Horam up distant signal in the background (depicted later in more detail), Fairburn 2-6-4T No 42105 leaves the station heading south for Hellingly with the 5.00pm Eridge to Eastbourne working on 23 April 1951. *J. J. Smith, courtesy Bluebell Railway Museum*

This is possibly the same coach set as seen earlier, but here being hauled by Class 'E5' 0-6-2T No 32406 on 22 April 1951. The location is near Horam, although it is not possible to pinpoint the exact spot. While sporting lined BR black livery, no further evidence of ownership is apparent. *J. J. Smith, courtesy Bluebell Railway Museum*

Again seen near Horam, on 23 April 1951, 'I3' 4-4-2T No 32083 dwarfs its two-coach train of former LBSCR stock. One point of interest is the number of headlamps stored on top of the loco's side tank. In the Horam area there was also a brickworks with its own internal narrow-gauge system. Logic would dictate that products might have been despatched by rail from the station, but there is a distinct lack of evidence on this point. *J. J. Smith, courtesy Bluebell Railway Museum*

Left: A former LBSCR signal post and arm still serve as the up distant signal for Horam on 23 April 1951. It was situated 800 yards from the corresponding up home signal and 1,097 yards from the platform signal box. As mentioned earlier, originally this would have been a worked arm, but was now fixed and thus would display caution at all times regardless of the state of the stop signal. The guy wires may also be noted. *J. J. Smith, courtesy Bluebell Railway Museum*

Below: This delightful portrait of Billinton Class 'C2X' 0-6-0 No 32434 on the 2.35pm freight from Tunbridge Wells West to Polegate was recorded near Horam on 23 April 1951. The engine, while displaying its painted BR number on the cabside, has yet to receive a smokebox numberplate. *J. J. Smith, courtesy Bluebell Railway Museum*

Hellingly

A first for this book, Maunsell three-cylinder 'U1' Class 2-6-0 No 31908 is seen near Hellingly with the 10.23am Tunbridge Wells West to Eastbourne service on 3 June 1956. The four-coach Maunsell set behind the engine, probably No 453, had originally been built for the London-Folkestone/Deal/Ramsgate services but was then superseded by more modern BR vehicles so was now seeing service on lesser duties. *J. J. Smith, courtesy Bluebell Railway Museum*

With Hellingly station in the background, super-power has been provided for the 9.25am Eastbourne to Tunbridge Wells West working on 3 June 1956. Certainly the train did not warrant two engines, 'C' Class 0-6-0 No 31583 and BR Class 4 No 76054, but this pathing duty would have been the most economic method of getting both to where they were needed for their respective next duties. *J. J. Smith, courtesy Bluebell Railway Museum*

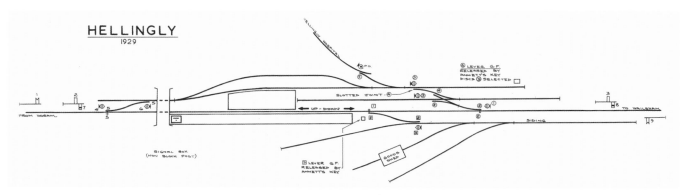

Signal box diagram, Hellingly.

One advantage of working for the railway was the ability to know when the more unusual workings were planned. Having this inside knowledge was the case here for the photographer, who has left his desk to record the passage of the annual weed-killing train over the Cuckoo Line on 3 June 1956, photographing it near Hellingly. No 31583 is seen again, but this time with 'K' Class 2-6-0 No 32346. We are not told if the 'C' Class loco took this train before or after the passenger working seen earlier. The spraying took place at the rear of the train. The tank cars contained the necessary chemical, which was gravity-fed through a series of pipes to the rear van. The weed-killing train would cover all running lines at least once a year, sidings and yards being the responsibility of the local permanent way gang, often using nothing more technical than a watering can. *J. J. Smith, courtesy Bluebell Railway Museum*

This is the main station building at Hellingly, the only station where there was no passing loop to enable trains to cross. There were, however, several sidings, and a signal box had originally been provided, although the location was a 'non-block post'. As a means of economy, the signalling was removed in 1930, all points being converted to hand operation, with those allowing access to and from the running line only able to be unlocked by means of an Annett's key attached to the train staff for the Horam to Hailsham section. *Terry Cole*

Hellingly was basically at the bottom of the bank, the formation having been falling most of the way since Heathfield. The line from Hailsham north had required some fifty bridges to be built but, unlike south of Hailsham, there were no public level crossings. Fairburn tank No 42068 is more than sufficient motive power for this three-coach set of BR Mk 1 vehicles in crimson and cream livery as it leaves Hellingly station for Hailsham – the 9.39am departure from Tunbridge Wells West – on 12 July 1959. *J. J. Smith, courtesy Bluebell Railway Museum*

With Hellingly station in the background, Drummond 'M7' 0-4-4T No 30031 leaves the station northwards on the climb towards Horam and Heathfield on 12 July 1959. The train is the 9.45am from Eastbourne, its eventual destination being Tunbridge Wells West. Assuming the service was running to time, departure from Hellingly would be at 10.06am. Note the overbridge built to span double track. As was practice, most single lines were built having sufficient land for doubling if this was later deemed necessary. Some, but not all, of the fixed structures on the Cuckoo Line were similarly constructed and at Hellingly this proved to be a useful asset, allowing a shunting neck for the hospital sidings at the north end of the site – see the next photograph. *J. J. Smith, courtesy Bluebell Railway Museum*

Below: Around the turn of the 20th century a private siding was provided by East Sussex County Council from Hellingly station to what was then referred to as the county lunatic asylum. This was then in the process of construction approximately 1¼ miles east of the railway. Initially Hellingly station was used simply as the point to which materials for use in the construction of the building were brought, then transferred to the site using a contractor's steam engine. However, upon opening what we would nowadays refer to as the hospital, arrangements were made for the line to be used not only for the transport of coal and other stores but also for the movement of staff, patients and visitors.

Unusually for the period, an overhead electric supply was used, and two electric locos were provided. The first of these is seen here and was used for the movement of coal and other materials from Hellingly station to and from the hospital site. The second was a tramcar-type vehicle that was used for passengers. Despite the demise of passenger services to the hospital in 1931, the small electric loco continued to be used for the movement of coal wagons – two at a time – until the hospital boilers were converted to oil in March 1959. Subsequently it was only in sporadic use until the railway facility was withdrawn c1960. In this view it is seen in operational use on 1 September 1951. *J. J. Smith, courtesy Bluebell Railway Museum*

From Station Road overbridge at the north end of the station we can obtain a good view of the site on what was a very wet Saturday 24 February 1951. The railway goods yard is on the west side of the line immediately south of the station and will be referred to in more detail with the next view. To the left are the interchange sidings for the hospital line: there was access to the running line at either end, while between the running line and the sidings had once been a wooden passenger platform used when there was occasion to transfer passengers from a service train to the tramcar to take them to the hospital. As mentioned above, passenger use ceased in 1931, although clearly it had taken some time to remove all traces of the platform. *J. J. Smith, courtesy Bluebell Railway Museum*

Viewed across the interchange sidings, we have a distant view of the station goods yard. The latter was not brought into use until 1890, initially with just two sidings; a third was added shortly afterwards in anticipation of additional traffic to the hospital. Visible in the yard is the flour shelter, which came second-hand from Battersea; it was provided because large quantities of flour were dealt with here, which had been processed by a mill at Horsebridge (about half a mile south of the station, and not to be confused with the station of the same name north of Romsey in Hampshire). Flour was a lucrative traffic for the railway but was lost to road transport in the 1950s. *Hugh Davies, 'Photos from the Fifties'*

Because of its almost unique character, there were several visits by enthusiasts to the hospital line in the 1950s, accommodation for 'passengers' being provided by a standard SR brake van. Here enthusiasts are working over the line on 1 September 1951. Another visit, recalled by Roger Holmes, was organised by the Railway Enthusiasts' Club, but on that occasion BR had forgotten to deliver the pre-booked brake van, which resulted in everyone having either to squeeze into the cab of the little loco or somehow attach themselves to the buffers. Roger commented that many in their party were wet through, having visited what was a blustery promenade at Eastbourne earlier in the day, and their predicament was not helped by a number of apparently live electrical components within the cab of the little engine… Current was taken from a 500V dc supply generated by the hospital, which also fed into the grid. The locomotive was of German manufacture and rated at just 14hp. In similar fashion to a tramcar, it was necessary for the collecting pole to be swung through 180° when changing direction. No signals were provided on the hospital line, all points being hand-operated and a key provided to unlock a gate protecting the line. *J. J. Smith, courtesy Bluebell Railway Museum*

This view of Hellingly and its yard connections was taken from the south end on 12 July 1959. Starting on the left we have the BR goods shed, flour shelter and corrugated store. Not so obvious on the left were coal staithes against the left-hand siding. The loading gauge is another item principally made of SR concrete. To the right of the flour shelter was a fixed 5-ton crane and a small goods shelter. On the right-hand side of the running line we can see the two-lever ground frame affording access to the hospital sidings. This was unlocked by the Annett's key on the train staff, after which one lever would unbolt the facing point lock and the second would then move the actual turnout. The train staff could not be removed until the points and lock had been restored to their 'normal' position – as seen here, set for the main line. Clearly little, if any traffic, is now passing over the hospital line – hard to believe that the hospital had its own weed-killing wagon, which would have been in regular use. To the extreme right, a line of overhead posts carrying the power supply indicates the course of the line towards the hospital, part of which was on a 1 in 50 gradient. *J. J. Smith, courtesy Bluebell Railway Museum*

On the same date, 12 July 1959, we have a closer view of the tramway sidings, and this time also a glimpse of the yard crane and goods shed referred to earlier. According to an article in the magazine *Railways* in 1951, an average of six loaded wagons of coal were handled each day from the main station to the hospital in the 1920s, reducing to four during the summer period. With the little electric locomotive only able to deal with two at a time, it can be seen that at least three trips daily would have been required, also assuming that the empties could be returned at the same time. *J. J. Smith, courtesy Bluebell Railway Museum*

'Working instruction, Hellingly: East Sussex County Asylum Private Siding – This siding leads from the down sidings east side of the station and is controlled by catch points and the disc signal worked from a ground frame. The asylum's private electric locomotive works vehicles to and from the siding as required under the supervision of the station staff. Trucks are placed on and taken from the electric siding by the engine of the ordinary goods train services.'

With the station yard not having seen any traffic for some time, Standard Class 4MT No 80084, but devoid of its front number plate, leaves the station for Hailsham with the 6.52am Tunbridge Wells West to Eastbourne service on 12 June 1965, the last day of public operation. *J. J. Smith, courtesy Bluebell Railway Museum*

A week or so prior to the last view, on 4 June 1965, sister engine No 80141 arrives at the station northbound. Of interest here is that all traces of the hospital line have been obliterated by this time, while the train would also seem to lack interest for any potential passengers. *Hugh Davies, 'Photos from the Fifties'*

A concluding view of Hellingly shows the body of the former hospital railway passenger tramcar now grounded and modified as the hospital sports pavilion. The underframe and axles were used for the construction of an internal-user 5-ton wagon. Having survived for almost 70 years, it would eventually meet a sad end when destroyed by fire at the hands of vandals. *Roger Thornton, Noodle Books collection*

Steam and a spring meadow. 'C2X' No 32543 is photographed near Horsebridge with a Tunbridge Wells West to Polegate freight working on 22 June 1951. *J. J. Smith, courtesy Bluebell Railway Museum*

Near the same location, another 'C2X', this time No 32434, is in charge of the 2.35pm Tunbridge Wells West to Polegate on 10 May 1951. *J. J. Smith, courtesy Bluebell Railway Museum*

The location of Leaps Cross (sometimes Leap's Cross) was north of Hailsham, the down (worked) distant for which is seen above the train. The service is unusual, being the 7.15pm Eastbourne to High Brooms (near Tunbridge Wells) special, which ran on 16 August 1950. Motive power for what appears to be a ten-coach working was provided by 'D' No 31733 and 'Q1' No 33033. *J. J. Smith, courtesy Bluebell Railway Museum*

Disgustingly dirty 'E' Class 4-4-0 No 31315 passes Leaps Cross in charge of the 4.39pm Eastbourne to Tunbridge Wells West passenger working on 7 April 1951. It is hard to imagine that 40-odd years earlier this engine would have been as clean as possible, charged with working the principal passenger services on the former South Eastern & Chatham Railway main lines from London to the North and East Kent towns. *J. J. Smith, courtesy Bluebell Railway Museum*

In this view at Leaps Cross before we reach the final Cuckoo Line station of Hailsham, a single coach is all that is required for this service, the 6.40pm 'short working' from Waldron to Eastbourne on 5 April 1951 behind 'E4' 0-6-2T No 32480. Note the apparent lack of any headcode or lamps.
J. J. Smith, courtesy Bluebell Railway Museum

Hailsham

Hailsham down distant signal, photographed on 21 April 1951, was a mechanically worked arm 1,432 yards from the signal box and 1,000 yards in rear of the down home signal. It was a former LBSCR wooden post signal slightly unusual in having the balance weight part way up the post. The arm is wooden and is clearly showing the effects of age, hence the two vertical metals strips holding the timber together. The single electric cable at the top of the post is the connection to a lamp 'in-out' repeater in the signal box. Should the oil lamp be extinguished, a warning bell would sound in the signal box to alert the signalman.
J. J. Smith, courtesy Bluebell Railway Museum

Pull-push working on the Cuckoo Line: the 4.10pm 'short working' from Polegate to Hellingly is seen near Hailsham on 28 April 1951. Pushing from the rear is 'D3'

0-4-4T No 32385, at the time 58 years old and due to survive to be just 60 before being taken out of service. The two coaches form pull-push set No 650, which since 1934 had consisted of coaches Nos 6940 and 2087. The vehicle nearest the loco is a former LBSCR body on a new underframe. Originally allocated to work on the Westerham branch, the vehicles were later given a general 'South Eastern' allocation but, as depicted here, this was capable of wide interpretation. *J. J. Smith, courtesy Bluebell Railway Museum*

Below: Arriving at Hailsham from the south is 'C2X' No 32536 with a Polegate to Hailsham 'short working', the 5.34pm train, on 12 May 1953. The railway here is single track, the two set of rails on either side being headshunts – left for the down siding and right for the goods yard. The engine shows evidence of burning at the base of the smokebox door. *J. J. Smith, courtesy Bluebell Railway Museum*

Having arrived at Hailsham, No 32536 has run round and now sets off back to Polegate as the 6.18pm service. Working tender-first was not ideal for the crew but, with no turntable available, there was no option. Before setting off, the fireman will doubtless have dampened the coal considerably in an effort to minimise the level of dust. *J. J. Smith, courtesy Bluebell Railway Museum*

A train we have seen before at different locations, the 2.35pm freight from Tunbridge Wells West, was recorded at Hailsham on 18 August 1950. It has set off 'bang-road' ('wrong line'), heading south from the up platform, although this was a signalled move indicated by the starting signal in the 'off' position at the end of the platform. One of two possibilities would have occurred: either the freight had been sidetracked to allow a down passenger train to pass, or it is just setting off after having shunted the yard, which is seen on the left. *J. J. Smith, courtesy Bluebell Railway Museum*

Viewed from across the goods yard in 1950, 'D3' 0-4-4T No 32385 is seen again leaving the station with another short 'pull-push' working back to Polegate. As may have been gathered, the platforms at Hailsham were staggered, that on the up side extending northwards. The main station buildings at Hailsham were on the down side – from where the train is leaving. Until 1880 Hailsham had been a terminus, and in those earliest days trains had been worked by examples of Craven-design 2-4-0 and 0-6-0 types, while after the opening north to Eridge it was in the main Stroudley designs that were in charge. Behind the down-side buildings a house for the incumbent station master was provided in 1892. *S. C. Nash, Stephenson Locomotive Society collection*

A mixed rake behind unique 'Baltic' tank Class 'J1' No 32325, formerly named *Abergavenny* (seen earlier at Tunbridge Wells West), leaves Hailsham for Polegate on 18 August 1950; the working is not recorded. Just behind the loco is Hailsham signal box, which contained 22 levers including one spare (No 4). In addition there was a second box operated as a ground frame/non-block post at the north, Hellingly, end of the up platform.
J. J. Smith, courtesy Bluebell Railway Museum

Pull-push set No 653 stands in the sidings at Hailsham on 17 June 1951 awaiting its next duty. Set No 653 consisted of two non-corridor former LSWR vehicles, carriages Nos 6429 and 2, and was in revenue-earning service until February 1961. Pull-push working on the Cuckoo Line had been used for some trains between Polegate and Hailsham from 1912 and over the whole line from 1922 onwards. After 1962 passenger trains were either DEMUs or formed of conventional locomotive-hauled stock. One private-owner wagon is known to have operated to and from Hailsham; this was for 'White & Beeny Coal Factors' and was in black livery with white letters, the latter shaded in green. *J. J. Smith, courtesy Bluebell Railway Museum*

Dating back to the time when the railway opened, when it was a terminus, these are the main station buildings at Hailsham with cars from the 1960s: l to r, a Morris 1000, Ford Anglia, Ford Popular and Wolseley. Note that the totems on either side of the station name still bear the legend 'Southern', notwithstanding that this is a March 1964 view, 16 years after nationalisation. *Noodle Books collection*

At the head of a three-coach Bulleid set, Standard Class 4MT No 80142 waits to leave Hailsham southbound in the last month of operation, June 1965. The photographers recording the scene bear witness to the sad occasion. On the right-hand side was a bay platform often used for 'short workings' between Hailsham and Polegate. *Hugh Davies, 'Photos from the Fifties'*

Signal box diagram, Hailsham.

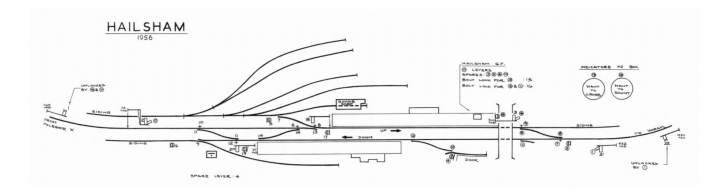

'Working instruction, Hailsham: Green & Burtenshaw's siding. This siding is connected by hand points with the south end of the down siding, the latter having been extended 560 feet. The new siding holds twelve wagons clear of the gate and the railway company's engines will place and draw from the siding loaded and empty wagons as required. The points must lie normally for the down siding. The key of the gate is kept at the signal box and the guard or shunter in charge must, after completing the work at the siding, lock the gate and return the key to the signal box. No movements must be made upon this siding after a down train has left Waldron, unless the facing points of the down line are set for the single line. The signalman on duty must instruct the shunter in charge as to the running of down traffic, when this is necessary. As a warning to men engaged at the brick yard and works, drivers must give one long whistle before entering and again before leaving. Trucks must not be allowed to stand on the down siding before or after shunting Messrs Burtenshaw's siding.'

'Working instruction, Hailsham: Stricklands' corn stores. Situate at extreme north end of No 1 goods road. Eight wagons can be dealt with at the firm's platform.'

Another single-coach working departing south, this time it is Maunsell 'U1' Class 2-6-0 No 31890 leaving Hailsham for Polegate in 1951. This engine only appeared regularly on Cuckoo Line trains for two spells in 1951, the first on Saturday 10 March with the 12.03pm from Victoria (turn 736), and the next on Thursday 15 March on the 6.10pm from Victoria, against which there is a note from Sid Nash: '4 carriages berthed Oxted (pt of 9.20 Eridge). No 31890 worked the 8.00 Brighton terminated at Oxted due to break away between 1st and 2nd coaches on leaving Oxted. 31890 terminated and worked empty to Victoria but did not reach there in time to work next train from Victoria at 12.03.' It was next seen on Thursday 22 March with the 3.52pm from Victoria (five corridors and a three-coach set, duty No 737); Saturday 21 April on the 4.18pm from London Bridge (duty No 740); Saturday 5 May, again with the 4.18pm from London Bridge; and finally on Monday 21 May on the 5.44pm Brighton to Tonbridge (duty No 753). *S. C. Nash, Stephenson Locomotive Society collection*

Some time in 1950 Fairburn tank No 42101 enters the station from the direction of Hellingly and passes an up train waiting to depart. The staggered platforms mean that the up service is fully alongside the platform. On the extreme right is the siding that led to a loading dock. *Hugh Davies, 'Photos from the Fifties'*

Sister Fairburn tank No 42102 heads south, this time seen from the up platform. Heading north, the single line commenced at the crossover just under the bridge, although there was also a long length of siding beyond this point. On the extreme left is the north ground frame and beyond, showing up well against the white-painted section of bridge, the up starting signal. This signal was 'slotted' in operation from both the signal box and the ground frame – as indeed were other items at the north end of the station. It also meant that train arrivals and departures at the north end were a complex and labour-intensive operation. *Hugh Davies, 'Photos from the Fifties'*

From the same position, 'I3' 4-4-2T No 32029 is seen arriving southbound in 1950, its last full year of operation.
S. C. Nash, Stephenson Locomotive Society collection

With apologies for the slight damage to the negative, we could not resist including this and the next view showing 'K' Class 2-6-0 No 32352 recorded on the 4.59pm Eastbourne to Hailsham service on 20 April 1957, arriving at Hailsham station. The home signal is a Southern upper-quadrant arm on a wooden LBSCR post, and was destined to be replaced soon afterwards. *J. J. Smith, courtesy Bluebell Railway Museum*

No 32352 has run round its train at Hailsham and is now on the way back to Polegate as the 5.20pm departure. This same engine and coaching stock was used for a further 'short working' later the same day, the 5.34pm Polegate to Hailsham, and finally the 6.15pm Hailsham to Eastbourne. Note the set number 346 on what is a modern three-car rake of BR Mk 1 stock. *J. J. Smith, courtesy Bluebell Railway Museum*

Colour at Hailsham: an unidentified 'Mogul' awaits departure south for Polegate. In its earliest days as a terminus the site had included an engine shed, although following completion of the route engine requirements were generally filled from the depots at either Tunbridge Wells West or Eastbourne. With the closure of the Cuckoo Line as a through route in 1965, DEMU-operated passenger services continued to operate between Polegate and Hailsham, while goods traffic continued north as far as Heathfield. Both of these were finally withdrawn in 1968. *Gerald Daniels*

Heading north, Class 'J1' No 32325 nears Hailsham with the 5.56pm train from Eastbourne to Tunbridge Wells West on 5 June 1950. South of Hailsham towards Polegate the railway passed over three public level crossings, Mulbrook Farm Road, Otham Court Road, and Sayerland Road.
J. J. Smith, courtesy Bluebell Railway Museum

Travelling on 4 September 1950 near Hailsham 'H' Class
No 31182 is in charge.
J. J. Smith, courtesy Bluebell Railway Museum

Hailsham's up distant signal was a working arm 869 yards
from the signal box, and could only be cleared to 'off' if
both the up home and up starting signals were also in the
'off' position. Photographed on 7 April 1951, this was
another 'Brighton' relic, following the tradition of having
the access ladder at the front of the post. According to
former Southern Region S&T Engineer Richard (Dick)
Brown, many if not all the distant signals on the Cuckoo
Line were replaced by colour lights in the period May to
September 1962. In addition, a number of dc track circuits
were installed, but not commissioned into use.
J. J. Smith, courtesy Bluebell Railway Museum

Further down the line and with two vans in tow, perhaps for milk, poultry or even flour, 'H' Class 0-4-4T No 31309 is working the 5.56pm Eastbourne to Tunbridge Wells West train on 22 July 1952. *J. J. Smith, courtesy Bluebell Railway Museum*

Rebuilt 'West Country' No 34008 *Padstow* is at the head of the 8.16am Eastbourne to Hailsham 'short working' on 6 August 1960. This was for many years a fill-in turn for the 'Pacific' and hardly likely to put any strain on engine or crew. Note that the carriages are of LMS origin.
J. J. Smith, courtesy Bluebell Railway Museum

In the reverse direction, the same engine and same stock are seen running as the 8.44am Hailsham to Eastbourne. The engine has clearly taken on coal before leaving Eastbourne and, with little effort required, not much has been consumed. Some of those lumps must have been close to the limit for the loading gauge! *J. J. Smith, courtesy Bluebell Railway Museum*

One week earlier on 30 July 1960 the same engine had again worked the early-morning train to Hailsham. The combination is seen here just north of Polegate, this time with a pair of Southern coaches but with coal that appears to be piled even higher. At the time, one would have had to travel to Southern lines west of Exeter, known collectively as the 'Withered Arm', to find one of the other few places where a big engine might be regularly seen on a train consisting of one or two coaches. *J. J. Smith, courtesy Bluebell Railway Museum*

Polegate

Having departed from Polegate some time in 1950, 'I3' No 32080, its last year of service, is seen on the first few yards of the Cuckoo Line heading towards the first station at Hailsham. *S. C. Nash, Stephenson Locomotive Society collection*

Another 'short working', this time a train operating between Heathfield and Polegate, is seen on 21 September 1952. It is hauled by the first-built Standard Class 4MT, No 80010 (Brighton, 1951), piloting Maunsell 'U1' Class 2-6-0 No 31906 near Polegate with the 11.39am working. *J. J. Smith, courtesy Bluebell Railway Museum*

Bulleid 'Q' Class 0-6-0 No 30534 is seen near Polegate in 1950. Sussex was an area where members of this class were relatively common on passenger workings, although elsewhere on the Southern they tended to stick to the freight duties for which they were designed.
S. C. Nash, Stephenson Locomotive Society collection

In last view of a branch train, we see SR Class 'E5' 0-6-2T No 2573 (later BR No 32573), also near Polegate in 1950. Between Hailsham and Polegate there was a private siding into the premises of the Maidenhead Brick & Tile Company. *S. C. Nash, Stephenson Locomotive Society collection*

'Working instruction, Polegate: Polegate Brick and Tile Co's siding. This siding is situated on the up side of the single line between Polegate and Hailsham, about 1¼ miles from the former station, with facing points as approached from Polegate. The points are worked from a ground frame on the down side of the line and the frame is controlled by Annett's patent lock, the key of which is fixed on one end of the staffs for this section of the line. There are two sidings, each holding five trucks, and inward trucks must be placed on one and the outward trucks taken from the other. There is a siding running from the south end of these sidings to the brick and tile works but the railway company's engines must not run upon this siding. Drivers must sound the whistle before entering the sidings from the main line and guards and drivers must keep a good look-out to see that no trucks are foul of the brick sidings and that no movement is being made thereon by the brick and tile company's men. All traffic for the siding must be labelled to Polegate for the Polegate Brick and Tile Co's siding, but as the siding is served by down ordinary goods trains, only such traffic must be worked via Hailsham. The gate at the company's boundary must be kept closed when the siding is not in use.'

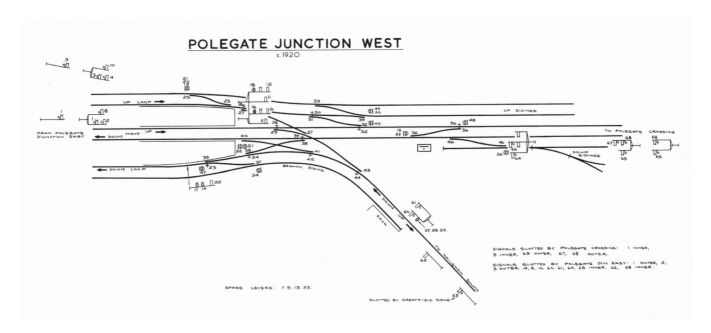

Signal box diagram, Polegate Junction West.

The Cuckoo Line proper ended at Polegate Junction West although, as will have been gathered, most trains continued to or originated from Eastbourne, the junction for which was at the opposite end of the station. Here we see the Cuckoo Line junction signal box and the branch towards Hailsham curving away to the right behind the goods yard, while straight on is towards Lewes. Polegate station, which is behind the photographer, consisted of two island platforms with all faces accessible to Cuckoo Line trains – hence the complex pointwork seen in this 30 November 1926 view. *David Wallis*

At the opposite end of the site, this is Polegate Junction East, with the lines to Eastbourne diverging to the right and those straight ahead to Hastings, also photographed on 30 November 1926. *David Wallis*

Signal box diagram, Polegate Junction East.

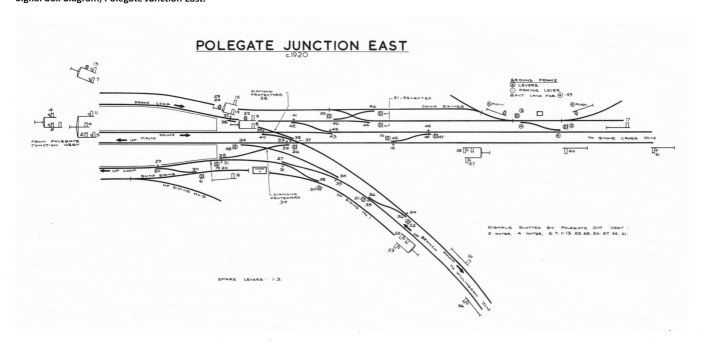

As mentioned in the Introduction, the original connection from the Cuckoo Line at Polegate faced towards Lewes, but this was abandoned from 3 October 1881 when the new station was built and through running to Eastbourne without reversal became possible. Seen here in 1926 are the remains of the original connection looking towards Lewes, the old station long closed and the path and earthworks on the right the site of the original connection to the main line. The replacement station referred to in the two previous views had been built with access from what was then Swines Hill Road, although not surprisingly this was quickly changed to Station Road. *David Wallis*

With many Cuckoo Line services starting or ending at Eastbourne, the concluding view in this section of the book is of an inter-regional service to Walsall leaving Eastbourne behind BR Standard Class 4MT No 80016. However, this is not a Cuckoo Line train and instead is of the type of working described by former fireman/driver Keith Holland as a 'Birkenhead Flyer'. *P. J. Lynch*

Cuckoo Line Memories 3
Roy Townsend

Interviewed by David Vaughan

Roy Townsend started work at Knight's Nurseries in Hailsham at 14 years of age earning 25 shillings (£1.25p) a week. When he was 15 years old a relative, who worked on the Southern Railway, told him that he could get 36 shillings a week on the railway as a locomotive cleaner at Eastbourne. That was a big rise in pay for a young lad in those days and, with the added incentive of free travel provided by the railway, he jumped at the chance and started work at Eastbourne in September 1943.

The result of enemy action at Eastbourne in the early afternoon of 4 May 1942. The water tank has been torn asunder, although fortunately the signal box still stands. Other areas of the town were damaged in the same raid, which lasted just 4 minutes. Sadly, in that time there were a number of casualties including those at the railway station. *RCHS, Spence collection*

I put it to Roy that being a cleaner in a dirty smelly environment was a far cry from the horticultural job he previously had and that it must have seemed a bit harsh by comparison. His reply surprised me, bearing in mind the nature of job and the circumstances at the time: 'I have thoroughly enjoyed my life on the railway. They did me a favour when I got that job.'

Roy did not stay a cleaner for long; in less than a year he was made a trainee fireman. The war was the catalyst for this swift promotion, as a number of men had been called up from reserve regiments at the start of the war and others had voluntarily left to join up. In addition, there were those injured or worse because the Southern Railway was in the front line of enemy attacks. London stations and goods yards were the constant target of the Luftwaffe during the Blitz, and Eastbourne too had more than its fair share of what were called tip-and-run bombing raids. The engine sheds sustained a direct hit during a raid not long before Roy became a member of its staff, resulting in most of the main roof being blown off and a number of engines badly damaged. At the age of 16 Roy was spared the brown envelope containing his call-up papers as by this time being a railwayman was considered of such importance that it was categorised as a Reserve Occupation.

The passenger station fared little better following the noon raid of Wednesday 16 September 1942. The effects of blast are apparent and it is known there was much damage to a train that was standing in the station. *RCHS, Spence collection*

Despite losing the roof over the engine storage and pits, the main building remained intact. This was a long block that consisted of rooms for the fitters, drivers, firemen and cleaners, as well as for the stores. Here was where the cleaners would collect their materials and the drivers and firemen obtain oil and other supplies. The clerks and the foreman also had their own offices. In the mess there was a large fire; Roy remembers that fire with some fondness, as he told me.

'You were never cold, even in the hard winters, like that of 1947. The fire had a large grate with fire bars like a railway engine and bars in front to stop the coal falling out of the hearth. We use to build it up till it roared like a furnace. Of course we used best steam coal for the fire and it was always kept alight 24 hours a day. Eventually I remember they had to rebuild it because the firebricks had all burned out!'

Eastbourne shed had a good complement of engines, mostly 'D' and 'E' Class ex-LBSCR tank locomotives designed by Marsh or Billinton for use on local goods and passenger services. Most of the larger passenger classes, such as the famous Brighton 'Atlantics', were stabled at Brighton and the new CME of the Southern, Mr Bulleid, had not yet started to build his 'light Pacifics'. There were, however, frequent visits by larger engines laying over from long-distance work. These were mainly used for goods turns, as the holiday excursion traffic had stopped during the war. Roy remembers that they also had a tender engine referred to as a 'Vulcan' – more accurately a 'C2X' type, so named as some had originally been built by the Vulcan Foundry.

Roy's early firing turns were confined to shunting the yard and the long siding known as 'The Duke's' that led to several local coal and timber yards and also served the local electricity and gas works. This line had previously extended to an area known as

'The Crumbles', which comprised a large acreage of shingle stretching from the eastern boundaries of the town as far as Pevensey Bay. This area was part of the estates of the Duke of Devonshire, hence the siding's nickname, and once supplied ballast to the LBSCR. The facility had closed in the 1930s, when the Southern Railway started to acquire granite ballast from its own large quarries at Meldon near Okehampton in Devon.

This long siding necessitated crossing several roads, and the locomotive crew was responsible for opening and closing the crossing gates. Trains of coal for the gasworks consisted of around 20 wagons and return trains consisted of coke from the work's own coking plant. There was also coal for the local 'Destructor' works, a plant for incinerating local household and industrial waste. Roy got a lot of useful practice on this line with shunting and also on local goods turns, before graduating to occasionally working night-time goods runs to Three Bridges. For that run, Roy booked on at 2.45am and made ready a loco that already had a fire lit in it. He and his driver then went light engine to Lewes and picked up a mixed goods train from the yard near Southerham Junction.

'We always had a tender engine for that job because it was a heavy train. Occasionally it was a War Department (ROD) locomotive and they were good powerful engines.'

I asked Roy if he had a favourite engine or class of locomotive. 'No, they were all good if you knew how to look after them. The trouble was, most of the engines I worked on were quite old; in fact, by the time the war ended they were clapped out and hadn't had a lot of maintenance during the war years.'

'I've heard it said,' Roy continued, 'and I quite agree with it, that steam engines are like women; they can be very temperamental and contrary. They were all different one from another; in fact, no two locomotives, even of the same class, were, in my experience, the same.'

I asked Roy about the tarpaulin that had to be rigged between the cab roof and the tender to act as a blackout, so that the glow from the firebox could not be seen from enemy aircraft.

'Well, it was pretty useless as far as that goes,' replied Roy. 'It was difficult to cut out the glare altogether and when the engine was working hard sparks would come out of the chimney, and as you were firing a shaft of light went right up to the clouds. The best that could be said is that it kept the rain off at least!'

I asked him what the drivers he worked with were like. I heard that some of them had a reputation for being less than helpful to a new fireman.

Roy replied, 'Yes, that's true. If the driver didn't show you what to do or give you any tips, you had to learn the hard way.

Mind you, you very soon caught on the right way to do things or else you'd be in trouble. One thing you learned quite quickly was that every time you fired you had to sweep the floor. I remember one driver, his name was Coombs, who was very particular and always had clean overalls. Woe betide if you hit his shoes or overalls with a lump of coal! He would tell you in no uncertain terms to sweep up. It all came as second nature in the end. The challenge was to keep on top of her [the engine], to keep the water level up, the fire nice and even and the steam pressure up to the mark without blowing off too much. Mind you, like I said, they were all different and some of them were right cows! A lot depended on the quality of the coal you were using – that could vary quite a bit. Some coal was nice and hard – you only had to show it to the firebox and it burst into flame. Good Welsh steam coal was the best, but during the war demand for that was high and it wasn't always what we got. Other stuff, like the coal we got from Tilmanstone colliery in Kent, well, that didn't hardly have a decent lump in it. Other coal used to clinker up something shocking, You had to get the pricker out and rake it all through or else chuck it out the door.'

Roy rapidly built up his store of experience on the footplate and was promoted to 'passed fireman'. This meant that he got occasional turns as a driver on goods turns and even the odd local passenger working.

'It was funny, though – as soon as I'd passed all my exams and was passed out as a driver proper, I was straight back on goods turns.'

The year 1948 brought nationalisation to a very run-down and undercapitalised railway system. There were changes afoot, apart that is from the obvious ones like the new so-called 'cycling lion' BR emblem on tenders and carriages. Roy soon found himself in charge of one of the LMS-designed Fairburn 2-6-4 tank locomotives, which were the precursors of Riddles's new Standard Class tank locomotives soon to be built at Brighton. I asked Roy what he thought of the new engines.

'Oh, they were lovely. You didn't realise how bad the old engines had become until you got one of the new ones. They steamed well, there was a lot more room in the cab, and all the controls were easy to hand. The driver even had a decent seat and things were better for the fireman too. It was a shame that they came into service too late really, because they were scrapped long before they were worn out.'

'I often went up through Tunbridge Wells West. There was a tunnel at the end of the station and clearances were tight. There was not much room between the roof of the tunnel and the top of the chimney on the engines. You always had to make sure you had a good head of steam before pulling away from the station as you never wanted to fire as you were going through the tunnel for fear of a blow-back from the firebox. I remember once, when I was a fireman, we had an engine that must have been due for a washout. As we went through the hole it started to prime. The cab filled with exhaust fumes and water vapour. It very soon became suffocating and I had a job to breath. By the time we came to the end of the tunnel I was nearly on the floor. The poor driver was just as bad. I never did like going through that tunnel after that.'

Roy also recalled some delightful anecdotes of his working, one of which involved a pheasant, which is rightly regarded as a fairly slow and stupid bird that could not fly very fast. They were often found dead by the side of the line, where they had been hit a glancing blow by a passing train, having failed to get out of its way in time. However, Roy recalls one incident on the Cuckoo Line where a pheasant proved more than a match for the train.

'We were coming back from a short working to Heathfield via Hailsham. It was an early turn and we had picked up quite a few people who worked in Eastbourne on the way. We were running bunker first on a tank engine and suddenly my fireman shouted out, "Quick! Open the regulator!" We were on the downhill run between Heathfield and Horam, which ran through some pretty woods at this point. Anyway, I opened up the throttle and put on a bit of speed. "Faster, faster!" shouted my fireman, who was hanging right out of the cab as far as he dared.

'"Why?" I asked. "What's going on?"

'He did not reply so I stepped over to his side of the cab and saw a pheasant flying right alongside the engine. It was so close you could almost reach out and touch it. Indeed, the fireman was trying to do just that. He was actually trying to catch it by the tail or else hit it with the coal shovel. The bird was certainly giving us a run for its money, as by now I had put on as much speed as I deemed safe and we were rapidly approaching the next station. All of a sudden the pheasant saw its chance and veered off through a gap in the trees. The fireman had not got as much as a tail feather.'

'Another time I was working at night on an engineers train with a platelaying gang on the line between Hellingly and Horam. We were doing a bit of to-ing and fro-ing, dropping off stuff as I went, when one of the platelayers shouted out to me, '"Ere mate, you got a dead cow on the line back there."

'"No!" I said. "You're pulling my leg.".

'"I'm not, it's lying in the cess, dead as a dodo."

'Well, I went back up the line a bit and sure enough there it was. It must have got out through a fence and couldn't find its way back. I never remembered hitting it so I must have just struck it a glancing blow. It probably didn't know what happened to it. Anyway, the foreman of the gang told the farmer about it next day and I never heard any more about it. It was the railway's responsibility to keep up the fences alongside the track but it wasn't their fault if the farmer had left a gate open to the next field. The farmer probably got some compensation for his dead cow but it was all sorted out quite easily. There was not all the hoo-ha and fuss that there would be nowadays.'

Another incident on the Cuckoo Line that sticks in Roy's mind was when they had a runaway.

'We were coming down from Heathfield to Horam. Nearer Horam there was a 1 in 50 downgrade and all of a sudden the driver I was firing to at the time shouted out, "Put the bloody handbrake on – we're away!" I wound on the handbrake as tight as I could and started to pull on the whistle and sound what we called the "Cock-a-doodle-do". That was the signal to tell those down the line that you were in trouble – you sounded it repeatedly. By that time we were about a mile north of Horam where we were due to stop and shunt as we had a train of unfitted goods wagons. The signalman heard us and set the points for straight through and we sailed on through and out the other side, where we stopped on a slight upgrade in a cutting. I can't tell you how glad I was when we stopped because there was nothing you could do about it if that happened. The guard had put his brake full on but we were still helpless. In the days before fully fitted freights were the norm there was nothing between you and the guard's brake. Sometimes, if you had a heavy train, you would stop at the top of a steep grade and the guard would pin down the brakes on a few of the wagons, but this was not the case if you were on a short branch-line train as we were. We were just lucky there was nothing approaching Horam from the other side.'

Time was running out for steam and Roy was sent to retrain on diesel locomotives. He completed his training and told me he found the transition easy. He was one of the first drivers to take the three-car diesel sets up from Lewes to Victoria on the Oxted line. They had three sets linked together for the rush-hour trains, he remembers.

'They were powerful enough all right, but boy were they noisy with that big diesel engine right behind the cab.'

Later on, Roy retrained again to drive electric trains, starting in 1966. In fact, he spent 26 years of his working life mainly on electrics. There were several types in use on the main lines to London and on the coast routes, and Roy drove them all.

'They were quite straightforward but there was no feeling to them. It was a job and you just got on and drove them. Not at all like the steam engines, which somehow felt alive. You had to work 'em. They were a challenge and you had a sense of achievement when you'd finished a turn of duty.'

Closure

Above: The Cuckoo line was listed for closure in Dr Beeching's infamous report *The Reshaping of Britain's Railways*, released in 1963. Despite some local opposition, there was in reality no solid justification at the time against closure, emotional campaigns being unlikely to curry favour with government. In reality there was simply not enough money to go round and sacrifices had to be made if the major routes were to survive and modernisation pushed through. The result would be closure. Before this took place, a number of enthusiasts' special workings were run in the last years. One was the LCGB (Locomotive Club of Great Britain) 'Wealdsman' circular tour on Sunday 13 June 1965 from London Waterloo and back via Wimbledon, Horsham, Crawley, Three Bridges, Rowfant, Eridge, Heathfield, Hastings, Eastbourne, Polegate, Haywards Heath, Steyning, Horsham, Cranleigh, Guildford, Cobham, Surbiton and Waterloo. Motive power at the start was Bulleid 'Pacific' No 34050 *Royal Observer Corps*, followed by two 'Moguls', 'N' Class No 31411 and 'U' Class No 31803, No 34050 again, and finally a brace of 'Q1s', Nos 33006 and 33027. The tour included travel over the length of the Cuckoo Line and the Horsham to Guildford line (the latter via Cranleigh), both of which had formally closed to all traffic the day before. Despite a schedule of 230 miles, numerous photographic stops (on the Cuckoo Line these were at Heathfield and Hellingly), together with the need to change engines and reverse directions on occasions, the tour ran almost exactly to schedule, departure from Waterloo being just 1 minute late at 9.54am, with the return reported also 1 minute late at 9.02pm. It was 'a grand day out', although tinged with sadness that the participants on the ten-coach train were the last fare-paying passengers to travel the length of the Cuckoo Line. The special is seen here on its way to Heathfield, complete with headboard, carriage roof boards and, for what was a sad occasion, perfect English summer weather. *Hugh Davies, 'Photos from the Fifties'*

Right: Obviously not everyone felt too depressed! *Trevor Owen*

The Licensing Magistrates have granted us a
SPECIAL EXTENSION
from 2pm on
Sunday. JUNE 13
The Locomotive Club of Great Britain
will be running a
VINTAGE STEAM TRAIN
through Sussex and making a
PHOTOGRAPHIC STOP AT
HELLINGLY STATION
This will be a Great Occasion
for YOU and your FRIENDS to
Drown Your Sorrow
for the closing of the
CUCKOO LINE

Above: The day before, Saturday 12 June 1965, had seen the final public services with both steam and diesel units involved. Here Standard 4MT 2-6-4T No 80144, complete with wreath and photographers, is recorded near Rotherfield. This service was a BR-sponsored 'Last steam trip' of six coaches and was well supported.
J. J. Smith, courtesy Bluebell Railway Museum

Meanwhile, at Mayfield a wreath had been prepared and is seen here prior to being attached to the front of a down DEMU service, also on the last day. The service was delayed somewhat as a large party of flag-waving residents travelled on the train as far as Heathfield: how they returned home again is not reported. Similar 'celebrations' were apparent at Horam for the final departure, the 10.24pm south from Heathfield, with an impressive display of fireworks and copious detonators exploding. This contrasted greatly with the departure of the same train from Heathfield, which had passed without notice. *J. J. Smith, courtesy Bluebell Railway Museum*

Three years earlier, on 24 June 1962, the Locomotive Club of Great Britain had run its 'Sussex Coast Limited' rail tour from Waterloo to London Bridge, taking in a number of routes, one of which was the Cuckoo Line. Preserved Drummond 'T9' 4-4-0 No 120 together with 'M7' No 30055 worked from Eastbourne to Rotherfield, where the 'M7' was detached, leaving No 120 to continue to East Grinstead and eventually London Bridge. The two steam engines are seen entering Rotherfield station just 4 minutes late at 7.01pm; a southbound DEMU is waiting for the special to clear the section south. *Dick Brown collection*

Some of the crowd from the train are recorded taking their own photographs during the 10-minute stop-over. Note especially the condemned wagons in Rotherfield goods yard. *Dick Brown collection*

There will be no more trains into or out of the tunnel at Heathfield, but it is still open to walkers as part of the East Sussex-funded 'Cuckoo Trail'. *Jeffery Grayer*

Goods traffic, mainly coal, continued to be handled at Heathfield until 1968, after which this station too was derelict. Much of the yard was subsequently redeveloped as an industrial estate, while at road level the former station buildings found a new use as a café and bookshop. *Jeffery Grayer*

Track-lifting at Hailsham occurred in the early 1970s, after which it would be a decade before further change occurred, the considerable station site now given over to housing. *Jeffery Grayer*

It was almost as if the demolition contractors had been sympathetic to the history of Horam as, apart from the lack of track, the station appears to be slumbering. Later there would be a rude awakening when the canopies were torn down and much of the site was given over to a new housing development. However, the 'Cuckoo Trail' is accessible here, with one of the former station running-in boards still in use providing information. *Jeffery Grayer*

South to Hellingly, where between 1965 and 1968 the station would awaken three times a week as a freight for Heathfield rumbled through. On the other two days, the freight would only run as far north as Hailsham. It was a far cry from the hourly passenger service introduced in 1956. Note the improvised washing line between the canopy supports. *Jeffery Grayer*

For a time a diesel shuttle service worked between Polegate and Hailsham, but economy had also seen this remaining service operate on the basis of 'one engine in steam', meaning that much of the signalling could be removed. Here a two-car DEMU waits amidst rusting track and a decaying station ready to return to Polegate. Despite the lack of any obvious patronage, the reverse would apply when services were finally withdrawn in April 1968. Then the station came alive for the final train, which departed with a complement of 150 passengers and a chorus of 'Auld Lang Syne' sung to the accompaniment of exploding detonators and the diesel's horn. *Jeffery Grayer*

Following passenger closure, the line lay moribund from Redgate Mill Junction through the former Rotherfield & Mark Cross and Mayfield stations as far south as Heathfield. This section of line was completely abandoned, for there would be no reprieve. Eventually the assets were sold off and the scrap contractors moved in. However, unlike on some other lines, the station buildings were not demolished and that seen here at Rotherfield was converted into private accommodation. The trackbed at Mayfield now sees a different type of traffic on what is now the village bypass. *Jeffery Grayer*

Meanwhile elsewhere things were not exactly rosy. Shorn of much of its traffic, the situation for the section from Eridge to Tunbridge Wells West hung in the balance. The end would come here on 6 July 1985, although there is some hope of a revival under the auspices of the Spa Valley Railway. Tunbridge Wells West steam shed also still stands, although it had been closed as an operational depot at the same time as the trains ceased on the Cuckoo Line. *Jeffery Grayer*

Line diagrams
Line curvature and gradients

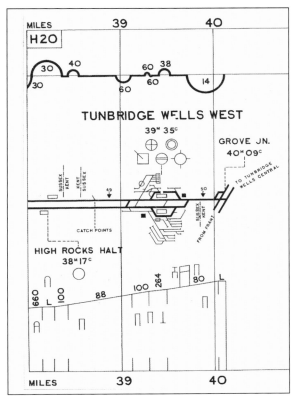

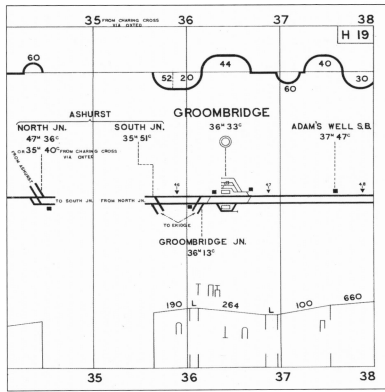

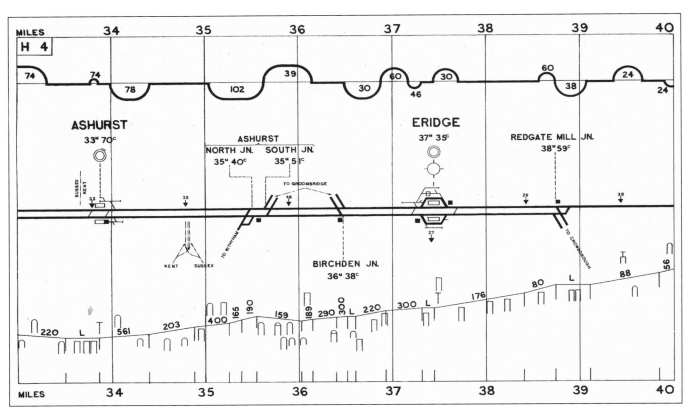

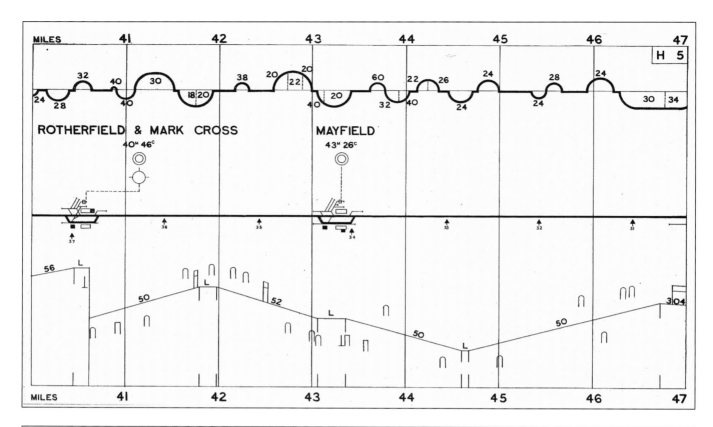

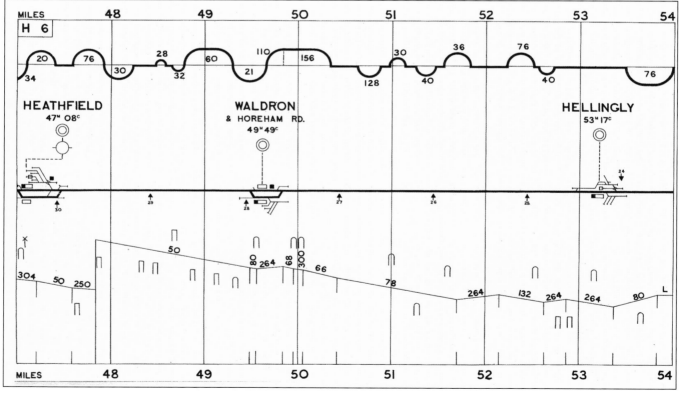

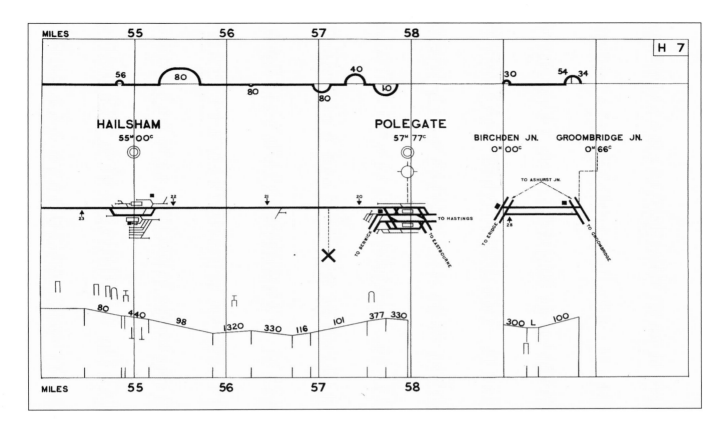

Specimen public timetable
September 1963 to June 1964

DOWN trains

Weekdays		am	am	am	am	am	am/pm	pm	pm	pm	pm	pm	pm	pm	pm
Tunbridge Wells West	dep		6.25		8.41	9.41	11.39		1.41	3.39		4.39	5.30		6.08
Groombridge	dep		6.31		8.47	9.47	11.44		1.47	3.45		4.45	5.36		6.14
Eridge	arr		6.35		8.47	9.52	11.49		1.51	3.5		4.5	5.41		6.18
Eridge	dep		6.36		8.51	9.52	11.54		1.51	3.5		4.53	5.5		6.26
Rotherfield & Mark Cross	dep		6.45		9.04a	10.03	12.01		2	3.59		5.02	5.59		6.34
Mayfield	dep		6.53		9.14	10.11	12.08		2.08	4.07		5.1	6.07		6.51e
Heathfield	dep	6.32	7.04		9.24	10.24	12.24c	1.37	2.22a	4.22B		5.25a	6.17		7.01
Horam	dep	6.4	7.15A		9.32	10.32	12.3	1.45	2.32	4.32		5.34	6.33B		7.17c
Hellingly	dep	6.48	7.23		9.4	10.4	12.38	1.52	2.39	4.39		5.41	6.41		7.25
Hailsham	dep	7.05d	7.32a	8.44	9.45	10.45	12.42	2.07g	2.44	4.44	5.2	5.46	6.21	6.48	7.06
Polegate	arr	7.12	7.4	8.51	9.52	10.52	12.49	2.14	2.51	4.51	5.27	5.53	6.28	6.55	7.13
Polegate	dep	7.12	7.4	8.51	9.52	10.52	12.5	2.14	2.51	4.51	5.32	5.53	6.37	6.55	7.14
Eastbourne	arr	7.21	7.49	9.01	10.01	11.01	12.58	2.22	3.01	5.01	5.39	6.02	6.44	7.04	7.22

Additional Eastbourne arrival figures shown at lower left (further early/other services): 7.53, 8.37, 9.05, 9.58

Notes:

d	arr 11 minutes earlier	
A	arr 3 minutes earlier	
a	arr 4 minutes earlier	
c	arr 7 minutes earlier	
g	arr 10 minutes earlier	
B	arr 5 minutes earlier	
e	arr 8 minutes earlier	

Note: Hampden Park station between Polegate and Eastbourne has been deliberately omitted, although most trains did call.

Saturday services: 11 down trains from Tunbridge Wells plus 3 from Hailsham and 1 from Heathfield.

Sunday services: 6 down trains plus 1 from Heathfield.

UP trains

Weekdays		am	am	am	am	am	am	am	am/pm	pm	pm	pm	pm	pm	pm	pm	pm	pm	pm
Eastbourne	dep	5.38	6.40	7.36	7.53	8.16	9.00	9.45	11.45	12.45	1.47	3.45	4.47	4.59	5.21	6.00	6.22	6.43	7.47
Polegate	arr	5.47	6.50	7.45	8.00	8.25	9.09	9.54	11.54	12.54	1.56	3.54	4.56	5.08	5.30	6.09	6.30	6.47	7.56
	dep	5.52	6.50	7.45	8.00	8.3	9.09	9.54	11.54	12.54	1.56	3.54	4.56	5.08	5.34	6.11	6.40	6.52	7.56
Hailsham	dep	6.01	7.00	7.51	8M22	8.38	9.16	10.01	12.01	1b07	2.02	4.01	5.03	5.14	5.4	6.18	6.46	6.56	8E11
Hellingly	dep		7.06	7.56	8.27		9.22	10.06	12.06	1.12	2.07	4.06	5.08			6.23		7.03	8.16
Horam	dep	6.14	7.13	8.04	8.36		9B35	10.16	12.14	1.2	2.14	4.14	5.16			6.31		7.08	8.23
Heathfield	dep	6.22	7.21	8.11	8.45		9.43	10.24	12.23	1.27	2a25	4.23	5.23			6.38		7.16	8A34
Mayfield	dep		7.32	8.22	8.56		9.53	10.34	12.34		2.34	4.34	5.34			6.49		7.23	8.45
Rotherfield & Mark Cross	dep		7.40	8.3	9.05		10A05	10.43	12.43		2.42	4.43	5.43			6.57		7.34	8.54
Eridge	arr		7.49	8.38	9.13		10.14	10.52	12.52		2.50	4.52	5.53			7.06		7.43	9.02
Eridge	dep		7.49	8.39	9.26		10.23	10.56	12.52		2.55	4.53	5.53			7.14		7.52	9.02
Groombridge	dep		7.53	8.43	9.3		10.28	11.01	12.57		2.59	4.59	5.58			7.18		7.56	9.07
Tunbridge Wells West	arr		7.59	8.5	9.37		10.37	11.07	1.03		3.08	5.07	6.05			7.25		8.06	9.13

Saturday services: 14 up trains from Eastbourne plus 3 only as far as Hailsham and 2 only as far as Heathfield.

Sunday services: 6 up trains plus 1 only as far as Heathfield.

Notes:

M arr 15 minutes earlier

B arr 5 minutes earlier

A arr 3 minutes earlier

b arr 6 minutes earlier

a arr 4 minutes earlier

E arr 8 minutes earlier

Index

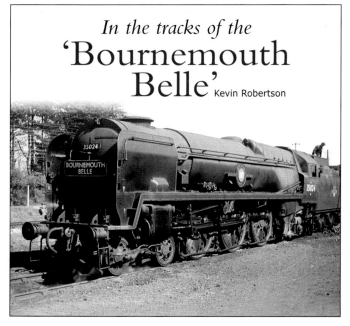

In the tracks of the
'Bournemouth Belle' Kevin Robertson

In the Tracks of the 'Bournemouth Belle'

Luxury train travel – Pullman style – was a feature of the railways until the 1970s and in the south several regular services bore the name Pullman. One, the 'Bournemouth Belle' was destined to become the last regular steam hauled train of its type to operate and served the Dorset town, running a daily service each way from Waterloo.

Apart from an interruption due to war, the train operated from the 1930s until the end of steam in the south in July 1967. Packed with fascinating facts and a plethora of images we see the service at its peak and in its decline and well as recording its passage throughout the route.

ISBN 9781909328556

Paperback, 128 pages **£12.95**